SIMON RICH is a gradua… president of *The Harvard Lampo…* a writer for *Saturday Night Live*. He … is currently writing and producing the hi… He lives in New York City.

PRAISE FOR *ELLIOT ALLAGASH*

"A sharp, clever, blisteringly funny debut." *The Times*

"*Clueless* for boys … suspect that, if he had a literary ancestor in mind as he charted Seymour Herson's rise, it was not Austen or [Amy] Heckerling, but Evelyn Waugh … studded with rococo set pieces of ruthless masculine one-upmanship … a joy to read … Open the book on the beach or by the lake, and shed a crocodile tear, if you can muster one, for the craven ambition of youth." *Daily Beast*

"A true original and incredibly readable … Funny, smart and generally bloody brilliant – read it." *Heat*

"A canny mixture of wish-fulfilment, fantasy and morality tale … The most enjoyable classroom comedy since Tom Perrotta's *Election*." *FT*

"If ever a book seemed custom-made for adaptation into a successful teen movie, the debut novel from *Saturday Night Live* writer Simon Rich is it. The plot is like that of the greatest film John Hughes never made: less Ferris Bueller's Day Off, more Ferris Bueller's Adolescence Off … a winning comic formula. Peppered with riotous teen angst – and effortlessly readable – this is a novel that one consumes like a pleasantly tangy packet of crisps." Tom Cox, *Daily Mail*

"Rich is intimately familiar with the subject, and nails everything. The novel is assured, deft in its rendering of teen relationships and, perhaps more remarkably, funny without resorting to the kind of gross-out humour common in this sort of setting. All laughs and no barfs, it's a breezy read." *G…*

PRAISE FOR *WHAT IN GOD'S NAME*

"Divinely funny" *Vanity Fair*

"One of the funniest writers in America ... Rich evokes enough of the hellish qualities of Earth (Lynyrd Skynyrd, Walmart, a screenplay for *Finnegans Wake*) and of the little things that we'll miss (Lynyrd Skynyrd, Walmart, a screenplay for *Finnegans Wake*) that it feels like a little love letter to the world. Thanks, life. Good of you to let me drop by." *Daily Beast*

"Truly hilarious" Eva Wiseman, *Observer*

"Hilarious and touching ... rest assured that you're in good hands here ... obviously Rich is crazy good at hysterical sharp dialogue. But the bonus here is that his head is matched by his heart. Rich lends the potentially gimmicky story real emotional heft and avoids condescending to his characters (or readers). At its best, *What in God's Name* reads like a screenplay for a film that might sit comfortably beside Woody Allen's early absurd works in a Netflix queue ... a clever, endearing novel." *Entertainment Weekly*

"*Elliot Allagash*, drew comparisons to Evelyn Waugh and P. G. Wodehouse. His new novel, *What in God's Name*, evokes another titan of English comedy: Douglas Adams ... Funny and occasionally touching, *What in God's Name* is satire that avoids sanctimony ... Rich knows how to balance the smart with the funny. When *What in God's Name* bares its teeth, it's because it's laughing." *New York Times*

"Rich's play on office politics and his understanding of the comic potential of human relationships is accurate enough, producing an appealing mixture of subtle and laugh-out-loud funny." *Independent on Sunday*

"Like Kevin Smith's *Dogma* via Neil Gaiman's *Good Omens*, it takes a lovingly satirical swipe at religion." *Grazia*

PRAISE FOR *THE LAST GIRLFRIEND ON EARTH*

"A collection of sweet stories full of whimsical, gently moving tales of love and loss, thwarted come-ons and doomed crushes ... Put it in your pocket and take it out whenever you need a five minute break from the tedium of everyday." *The Gloss*

"Most original and highly amusing. Rich manages to turn the banal into the absurd ... hilarious and touching ... and impossible to put down. A perfect cheer-up for the romantically challenged!" *Image*

"*The Last Girlfriend On Earth* is silly, surreal, sometimes sad and always laugh-out-loud funny. This collection will have you giggling/crying/squirming in recognition, and wondering what exactly Simon Rich has eaten to dream all this stuff up ... This collection pulls off the tough trick of being both heart-warming and hilarious – it's a must-read if you've ever so much as had a crush on someone." *Heat*

"Pithy, occasionally bonkers ... expect any weeping to be of the laughter-induced variety." *Time Out*

"A James Thurber for our times, in Borges' suit wearing Flann O'Brien's hat." Ian McMillan, *BBC Radio 3 The Verb*

"It would be almost a relief to find that *The Last Girlfriend on Earth* was another of those American humour collections by a writer falling short of their hype as an heir to David Sedaris and James Thurber, just to be reassured that Rich wasn't good at *everything*. As it happens, it's brilliant: a kind of modern version of Woody Allen's *Without Feathers* for anyone who's been in love ... Only a couple of times within the next 29 pieces does Rich hit a note that's not either topsy-turvy imaginative, riotously funny or hugely insightful ... Beneath the clear ambition to make people laugh, there's another book lurking here: a guide to the idiocy and sensitivity of men that could be more valuable to the opposite sex than a million 'How To Please Him' women's mag articles. Rich has a wisdom about male-female interaction that most have to wait far, far longer than 28 years to gain." Tom Cox, *Observer*

THE WORLD *of* SIMON RICH

The World of Simon Rich is drawn from *Free-Range Chickens* and *Ant Farm*, as well as uncollected pieces, which have appeared in *The Occasional* and *Observer Magazine*.

First published in Great Britain in 2016 by
Serpent's Tail,
an imprint of Profile Books Ltd
3 Holford Yard
Bevin Way
London
WC1X 9HD
www.serpentstail.com

1 3 5 7 9 10 8 6 4 2

Designed and typeset in Garamond by MacGuru Ltd

Printed and bound by CPI Group (UK) Ltd, Croydon CR0 4YY

A CIP record for this book can
be obtained from the British Library

ISBN 978 1 78125 748 7
eISBN 978 1 78283 308 6

Contents

Animals

Going to work

Relationships

Daily life

God

Growing up

Terrifying childhood experiences

– Got your nose!
– Please just kill me. Better to die than to live the rest of my life as a monster.

– What's that in your ear? Hey– it's a quarter!
– Why is everybody laughing? I have a horrifying brain disease.

– Peek-a-boo!
– Jesus Christ. You came out of nowhere.

A conversation at the grown-ups' table as imagined at the kids' table

MOM: Pass the wine, please. I want to become crazy.

DAD: Okay.

GRANDMOTHER: Did you see the politics? It made me angry.

DAD: Me too. When it was over, I had sex.

UNCLE: I'm having sex right now.

DAD: We all are.

MOM: Let's talk about which kid I like the best.

DAD: (laughing) You know, but you won't tell.

MOM: If they ask me again, I might tell.

FRIEND FROM WORK: Hey, guess what? My voice is pretty loud!

DAD: (laughing) There are actual monsters in the world, but when my kids ask I pretend like there aren't.

MOM: I'm angry! I'm angry all of a sudden!

DAD: I'm angry too! We're angry at each other!

MOM: Now everything is fine.

DAD: We just saw the PG-13 movie. It was so good.

MOM: There was a big sex.

FRIEND FROM WORK: I am the loudest! I am the loudest!

(Everybody laughs.)

MOM: I had a lot of wine, and now I'm crazy!

GRANDFATHER: Hey, do you guys know what God looks like?

ALL: Yes.

GRANDFATHER: Don't tell the kids.

A day at UNICEF headquarters as I imagined it in third grade

[UNICEF sits on a throne. He is wearing a cape and holding a sceptre. A servant enters, on his knees.]

UNICEF: Halloween is fast approaching! Have the third graders been given their little orange boxes?
SERVANT: Yes, your majesty!
UNICEF: Perfect. Did you tell them what the money was for?
SERVANT: No, sir, of course not! We just gave them the boxes and told them to collect for UNICEF. We said it was for "a good cause," but we didn't get any more specific than that.
UNICEF: Ha ha ha! Those fools! Soon I will have all the money in the world. For I am UNICEF, *evil king of Halloween!*
SERVANT: Sir ... don't you think you've stolen enough from the children? Maybe you should let them keep the money this year?
UNICEF: Never! The children shall toil forever to serve my greed!
[UNICEF tears open a little orange box and rubs the coins all over his fat stomach.]
UNICEF: Yes! Oh, yes!
SERVANT: Wait – your majesty! Look at this! Our records indicate that there's a kid out there – Simon – who's planning to *keep* his UNICEF money this year.
UNICEF: What?!? But what about my evil plans? I was going to give that money to the Russians so they could build a bomb!
SERVANT: I guess there's still one hero left in this world.
UNICEF: Noooo!
[Runs out of castle, sobbing.]
SERVANT: Thank God Simon is keeping his UNICEF money.
SECOND SERVANT: Yes, it's good that he's keeping the money.
THIRD SERVANT: I agree. Simon is doing a good thing by keeping the money from the UNICEF box.
SERVANT: Then we're all in agreement. Simon should keep the money.

When I lost my first tooth

ME: You're never going to believe this. I was hanging out with my friends and all of a sudden, a tooth fell out of my mouth. I think there's something seriously wrong with me.
MOM: Looks like the tooth fairy's coming to town!
ME: Who?
MOM: The tooth fairy. She visits children in the middle of the night and takes their teeth.
ME: Is she … a cannibal?
MOM: No, she's a fairy.
ME: What else does she take? Does she take *eyes*?
MOM: No, just teeth. And when she's done, she leaves a surprise under your pillow.
ME: Oh my God.
MOM: I wonder what it'll be this time?
ME: Okay … let's not panic here. There's got to be a way to trap her or kill her. We just need to *think*.
MOM: You don't want to kill the tooth fairy.
ME: Why not? Wait a minute … I see what's going on. You're in *cahoots* with her! God, it all makes sense now … how else would she know that I had lost a tooth in the first place?
MOM: I think someone's getting a little sleepy.
ME: Wait until Dad finds out about this!
MOM: He knows about the tooth fairy, sweetie.
ME: Jesus Christ. How high up does this thing go?
MOM: Let's get you tucked in.
ME: Listen … as long as we're laying it all on the line, you might as well be straight with me. What other fairies are you working with? Is there a *face* fairy?
MOM: There's just a tooth fairy, sweetie. She comes every time you lose a tooth.
ME: What do you mean "every time"? I'm going to lose more teeth?
MOM: You're going to lose all of them.

A conversation between the people who hid in my closet every night when I was seven

FREDDY KRUEGER: When do you guys want to kill him?
MURDERER FROM THE SIX O'CLOCK NEWS: How about right now?
DEAD UNCLE WHOSE BODY I SAW AT AN OPEN CASKET FUNERAL: I say we do it when he gets up to pee. You know, when he's walking down the hallway, in the dark.
FREDDY KRUEGER: What if he doesn't get up?
MURDERER: He'll get up. Look at how he's squirming. It's only a matter of time.
DEAD UNCLE: Man, I cannot *wait* to kill this kid.
MURDERER: Same here.
FREDDY KRUEGER: I've wanted to kill him ever since he saw my movie.
DEAD UNCLE: Hey, do you guys remember that night-light Simon used to have?
MURDERER: Man, that thing scared the heck out of me.
FREDDY KRUEGER: It's a good thing his mom got rid of it. Now there's nothing to stop us from killing him.
(Everyone nods in agreement.)
DR. MURPHY: Hey, guys, sorry I'm late. I was busy scheduling an appointment with Simon, to give him shots.
FREDDY KRUEGER: No problem.
(Freddy Krueger and Dr. Murphy do their secret handshake.)
MURDERER: It's getting kind of crowded in here. Chucky, can you move over?
CHUCKY: I'm over as far as I can get.
MURDERER: I need more space than you're giving me. I'm a lot bigger than you.
CHUCKY: Are you calling me *short?*
DR. MURPHY: Hey, guys, *relax,* all right? We're all here for the same reason: to kill and possibly eat Simon.

MURDERER: *(Sighs.)* You're right. I'm sorry.
CHUCKY: Yeah ... me too. I kind of lost perspective.
DEAD UNCLE: Hey, it looks like he's getting up! Wait a minute ... where's he *going!*
CHUCKY: I think he's running into his mom's room!
DEAD UNCLE: Maybe we should follow him?
CHUCKY: Are you *insane?* I'm not facing that kid's mother. That woman is terrifying!
FREDDY KRUEGER: *(Sighs.)* I guess tonight's a bust. Let's try tomorrow, okay? Same time, same place.

If adults were subjected to the same indignities as children

Party

ZOE: Dad, I'm throwing a party tonight, so you'll have to stay in your room. Don't worry, though: one of my friends brought over his father for you to play with. His name is Comptroller Brooks and he's about your age, so I'm sure you'll have lots in common. I'll come check on you in a couple of hours. *(Leaves.)*

COMPTROLLER BROOKS: Hello.

MR. HIGGINS: Hello.

COMPTROLLER BROOKS: So ... um ... do you follow city politics?

MR. HIGGINS: Not really.

COMPTROLLER BROOKS: Oh.

(long pause)

(Zoe returns.)

ZOE: I forgot to tell you: I told my friends you'd perform for them after dinner. I'll come get you when it's time. *(Leaves.)*

COMPTROLLER BROOKS: Oh God, what are we going to *do*?

MR. HIGGINS: I know a dance ... but it's pretty humiliating.

COMPTROLLER BROOKS: Just teach it to me.

Capitol Hill

LOBBYIST: If you fail to pass this proposition, it will lead to the deaths of thousands. Any questions?

SENATOR: Why are you wearing a sailor suit?

LOBBYIST: My children decided to dress me this way, on a whim. I told them it was an important day for me ... but they wouldn't listen.

SENATOR: It's adorable.

LOBBYIST: Okay ... but ... do you agree with the proposition? About the war?

SENATOR: Put on the cap.

Garage

ALBERT ROSENBLATT: Can I drive your car? I'll give it back when I'm done.

MRS. HERSON: I'm sorry ... do I know you?

ALBERT ROSENBLATT: No, but we're the same age and we go to the same garage.

MRS. HERSON: No offense, sir, but I really don't feel comfortable lending you my car. I mean, it's by far my most important possession.

PARKING ATTENDANT: Mrs. Herson! I'm *surprised* at you. What did we learn about sharing?

MRS. HERSON: You're right ... I'm sorry. Take my Mercedes.

ALBERT ROSENBLATT: Thank you. Can I come over to your house later? I'm lonely and I don't have any friends.

MRS. HERSON: Well ... actually ... I kind of had plans tonight.

PARKING ATTENDANT: Are you *excluding* him?

MRS. HERSON: No, of course not! *(Sighs.)* Here's my address, sir. The party starts at eight.

ALBERT ROSENBLATT: I'll show up a little early.

MRS. HERSON: What's that on your face?

ALBERT ROSENBLATT: Mucus. I haven't learned how to blow my nose yet, so I just go around like this all the time.

MRS. HERSON: Oh.

ALBERT ROSENBLATT: I'll see you soon, inside of your house.

I still remember the day I got my first calculator

TEACHER: All right, children, welcome to fourth grade math. Everybody take a calculator out of the bin.
ME: What are these?
TEACHER: From now on we'll be using calculators.
ME: What do these things do?
TEACHER: Simple operations, like multiplication and division.
ME: You mean this device just ... does them? By itself?
TEACHER: Yes. You enter in the problem and press equal.
ME: You ... you knew about this machine all along, didn't you? This whole time, while we were going through this ... this *charade* with the pencils and the line paper and *the stupid multiplication tables!* ... I'm sorry for shouting ... It's just... I'm a little blown away.
TEACHER: Okay, everyone, today we're going to go over some word problems.
ME: What the hell else do you have back there? A magical pen that writes book reports by itself? Some kind of automatic social studies worksheet that ... that fills itself out? What the hell is going on?
TEACHER: If a farmer farms five acres of land a day–
ME: So that's it, then. The past three years have been a total farce. All this time I've been thinking, "Well, this is pretty hard and frustrating but I guess these are useful skills to have." Meanwhile, there was a whole bin of these things in your desk. We could have jumped straight to graphing. Unless, of course, there's some kind of graphing calculator!
TEACHER: There is. You get one in ninth grade.
ME: Is this ... Am I on TV? Is this a prank show?
TEACHER: No.

Playing nice

Dear fourth grade parents,
In order to make sure no child gets hurt this year, the PTA has agreed to the following guidelines for birthday parties:

1. If a child invites more than half of the class, he must invite the entire class, including Ivan.
2. If a child only wants to invite a few best friends but Ivan hears that there's a party, that child must invite Ivan and pretend that the party is for Ivan.
3. If Ivan is at a party and he starts to have one of his fits, everyone else at the party (including parents) must pretend to have fits also so Ivan doesn't feel that he's the only one having a fit.
4. When Ivan runs out of steam, nobody should talk about what just happened.
5. If Ivan demands that a child invite him to a party, that child must invite Ivan to a party even if it's not that child's birthday and that child doesn't have any party planned. The next day, at the party, everybody should pretend that it actually *is* that child's birthday and Ivan was right about everything.
6. If Ivan figures out somehow that the other children have been faking their fits, the children must be taken out of school until Ivan has one of his major breakdowns and loses his recent memory.

No matter whose party it is, Ivan always blows out the candles and opens all the presents.

Thank you,
Mrs. Billings

Our thoughts are with you

Dear Mrs. Matthews,
I am writing to express my deepest sympathies. I shared your last note with Caleb's classmates and they made a card (which I have enclosed). Ten funerals in three weeks is a lot to ask of any child, let alone a child like Caleb, who has already suffered so many family deaths this month. At first, as humiliating as it is to admit, I thought your son had forged the notes. But denial quickly gave way to grief. I understand he has another funeral to attend on Wednesday and that it will last until Friday. Please let him know that he can take as much time off as he needs. I would volunteer to drop off Caleb's homework myself, but I understand that your house recently exploded. Of all the tragedies that have befallen your family, this one saddened me the most. For a house to suddenly explode, without warning, destroying a child's backpack and books, is very upsetting, particularly in the midst of your High Voodoo Holidays.

I was also deeply saddened to learn that your son had suffered brain damage and could no longer complete his social studies assignments. To be hit with such a misfortune, on top of Tourette's, is a blow to any child's self-esteem, especially when that child already has the plague.

Incidentally, I understand that Caleb has recently taken on some serious community service projects. I totally understand Caleb's devotion to the blind, particularly in light of his own blindness. But I'm worried that his extracurricular activities might interfere with his school-work, especially on top of the pressures of his upcoming Voodoo Bar Mitzvah. Of course, it's your decision.

I would also like to take this opportunity to congratulate you on your son's recent achievement! To be named an FBI super-spy at such a young age is an amazing accomplishment, particularly for a child who suffers from so many varied forms of brain damage. He hasn't told me much about his mission, but from what I gather it sounds like an incredible opportunity. I'm going to miss his presence in the classroom next year, but it would be selfish of me to stand in his way. Caleb's country needs him more than I do. He belongs in Russia.

Rest assured: I haven't told anyone about Caleb's mission, not even the principal. I am honoured that Caleb felt he could trust me with top secret information, and I would *never* betray that trust.

Godspeed,
Mr. Marks

Letters from camp

Dear Mom and Dad,
Camp is fine so far. They have a rule that after lunch you have to either write a letter to your parents or take a shower. I'm writing a letter. This place is pretty fun except it's so hot all the time that my skin sticks to my clothes.

Love,
Seth

Dear Mom and Dad,
I decided to write another letter, instead of the shower. The people in my bunk were like, "Come on, let's take a shower Seth, it'll be fun," but I knew you guys would want to hear from me! Things are okay except we play too many sports and it's hot and humid all the time.

Love,
Seth

Dear Mom and Dad,
Three letters in three days! You must be pretty excited to hear from me. Hold on, my counselor wants to write something. Hi, this is Craig Matthews, Seth's bunk counselor writing. I need to talk to you about a pretty serious situation. I can be reached day or night via cell phone at 917-490-3902. Hi – it's Seth again. I wonder what that's all about?

Dear Mom and Dad,
Another day, another letter! Nothing much to report. Having some trouble making friends. I'll write tomorrow.

Love,
Seth

Dear Seth's Mom,
Hi this is Jeff and Evan from camp we are in Seth's bunk we found your address by going through his things. Please tell your son to pick Shower instead of Letter tomorrow, we have a social with the girls' camp from across the lake.

Jeff and Evan

Dear Seth's Mom and Dad,
This is Debbie from Camp Swan I met your son at a dance and got your address from his friends. I think it's important that you know about what's going on. Please write to me soon.

Debbie

Dear Mom and Dad,
Greetings from the camp infirmary! I don't feel sick, but the counselors said I needed a rest. I'm pretty far away from all the activities, but its pretty fun here. Every few hours I get up and see how many jumping jacks I can do without stopping and once a day, someone comes by to pick up my letter. Hope you're enjoying Europe. I'll see you in August.

Love,
Seth

My mom's all-time top five greatest boyfriends

By Milo Farber, age 11

5. Jared Miller

This guy was awesome! He's by far the strongest, biggest dude I've ever met. But that's not all – he also plays for the Fort Wayne Warriors, my favourite minor-league hockey team! My mom dated Jared for a few days last summer, and every time he came to the house he gave me a regulation Fort Wayne Warriors hockey puck. By the end I had five pucks! Once I ran into him in the kitchenette in the middle of the night. He was making a sandwich. I couldn't believe there was a real hockey player in my house. I wanted to say something, but I was too nervous so I just stood there. Then after a while he looked at me and said, "Hey, little buddy. How's your skating?" And I said, "Fine!"

4. Olaf Seidenberg

Olaf wasn't as strong as Jared, but he was just as cool because he also played hockey for the Fort Wayne Warriors! He only dated my mom once, so I only had one chance to talk to him. Still, it was pretty awesome. It was in the middle of the night. I couldn't sleep, so I went to the kitchenette and *there he was,* Olaf Seidenberg, in *my* house! I asked him to sign my regulation pucks and he said he would. He couldn't believe I had so many pucks! "Wow, kid," he said, "you're a real fan." He autographed all five of them and wrote "16" next to his name, which is his number!

3. Martin Pavlovsky

This guy also played hockey for the Fort Wayne Warriors! He had four goals and two assists in 2006–2007, which isn't great but it was only his first year. When I asked him to sign my regulation Fort

Wayne Warriors pucks next to Olaf's signature, he made a weird scrunched-up face and stared at my mother for a while, like he was confused. I guess he doesn't understand a lot of English because he's from the Czech Republic.

2. Bill Passman

This guy played for the Fort Wayne Warriors. He was an okay goalie, but he had some bad luck so his save percentage was only *.899*. I liked him because his name has the word "Pass" in it, which is a hockey word – and he plays hockey. I only saw Bill once, in the kitchenette. I couldn't believe there was a real hockey player in my house! So I ran into my bedroom and grabbed the old cigar box I use to hold my pucks. When I came back with the box, my mother kept saying that I should go to bed. "Not now, Milo," she started shouting. "Please!" She can be really strict. Anyway, I could tell Bill wanted to see what was in the box so I opened it. "Wow," he said, "you must be my number one fan!" I gave him a puck and told him to sign it next to Olaf's and Nicolas's signatures. (Nicolas was another one of my mom's boyfriends, but he didn't make the top five.) At first he looked a little confused. He said something under his breath, and I was scared he wasn't going to sign my pucks at all. But then he took out a pen and signed *all of them!* It was weird, because he didn't look at the pucks when he signed them. Instead, the whole time he was staring at my mother. His signature was pretty cool – better than Nicolas's but not as good as Olaf's.

1. Bobby Lambert

This guy is great at hockey! He had forty points in the 2006–2007 season with my favourite hockey team, the Fort Wayne Warriors. He went out with my mom for almost two weeks. I didn't get to see him very often because my mom had made a rule that I couldn't leave my room when her boyfriends were over. Still, one night I decided to sneak out of my room and wait in the kitchenette. I mean, how many chances do you get to see a real hockey player in your own house?

When I showed Bobby my puck collection, he was super-impressed. "What the hell is going on?" he kept saying. "What the goddamn hell is going on?" Then he looked at my mom and started to cry! It was awesome because I always feel ashamed when I cry. But I thought, If a guy like Bobby Lambert can cry, an AHL all-star centre with thirty-five assists, then it's okay if I do too. Bobby kept crying and I was so blown away that I started crying too. And when I went over to him, he hugged me with his huge arms and it was like I had just scored a goal and he had given me the assist.

Math problems

UNIT 4 TEST
Please show your work.

1. A name-brand bottle of rum costs $12.95. The generic brand sells for $7.50. If a math teacher buys 4 bottles of generic rum each week, how much does he save each month? How much does he save each year? How much money does the teacher save over the course of 11 years?
2. A math teacher's new apartment is approximately 12 ft. long and 5 ft. wide, and the bathroom takes up 50% of the apartment. A normal human-size bed is 6 ft. × 3 ft. Does the math teacher have enough room for a standard bed? Or will he have to sleep in some kind of dog bed?
3. By order of the high courts, a math teacher must keep 1,000 ft. away from his ex-wife at all times. Say, theoretically, she lives on 63rd and York, exactly halfway between the math teacher's apartment and his school. How far out of his way does the teacher have to walk every morning just to keep from getting arrested?
4. After 11 years of service, a math teacher receives an $80 gift certificate to Shaw's Gas in lieu of a raise. How much of that money will be left after taxes? Express in bottles of rum.

Frogs

– Hey, can I ask you something? Why do human children dissect us?
– It's part of their education. They cut open our bodies in school and write reports about their findings.
– Huh. Well, I guess it could be worse, right? I mean, at least we're not dying in vain.
– How do you figure?
– Well... our deaths are furthering the spread of knowledge. It's a huge sacrifice we're making, but at least some good comes out of it.
– Let me show you something.
– What's this?
– It's a frog dissection report.
– Who wrote it?
– A fourteen-year-old human from New York City. Some kid named Simon.
– *(flipping through it)* This is it? This is the whole thing?
– Uh-huh.
– Geez ... it doesn't look like he put a whole lot of time into this.
– Look at the diagram on the last page.
– Oh my God ... it's so *crude.* It's almost as if he wasn't even looking down at the paper while he was drawing it. Like he was watching TV or something.
– Read the conclusion.
– *In conclusion, frogs are a scientific wonder of biology.* What does that even mean?
– It doesn't mean anything.
– Why are the margins so big?
– He was trying to make it look as if he had written five pages, even though he had only written four.
– He couldn't come up with one more page of observations about our dead bodies?
– I guess not.

– This paragraph looks like it was copied straight out of an encyclopedia. I'd be shocked if he retained any of this information.
– Did you see that he spelled "science" wrong in the heading?
– Whoa ... I missed that. That's incredible.
– He didn't even bother to run it through spell check.
– Who did he dissect?
– Harold.
– Betsy's husband? Jesus. So this is why Harold was killed. To produce this ... "report."
– *(Nods.)* This is why his life was taken from him.

(long pause)

– Well, at least it has a cover sheet.
– Yeah. The plastic's a nice touch.

I can only think of two scenarios where high school math would come in handy

1

MURDERER: I'm a crazy person. Do this trigonometry problem or I'll murder you.
ME: Can I use a graphing calculator?
MURDERER: Yes, of course. Oh – and here's a list of necessary formulas.
ME: Great, thanks. Okay, let's see ... $\sin 2x = 2\cos x \sin x$?
MURDERER: That's correct. You're free to go.

2

OLD RICH MAN: Hello, everyone. I've gone completely insane. Whoever solves this trigonometry problem fastest gets all of the money in my will.
ME: Can we use graphing calculators?
OLD RICH MAN: Yes – and the necessary formulas are on the second page.
ME: Cool. Is it $t = 50$?
OLD RICH MAN: I need it expressed to me in radians.
ME: $t = 0.28$?
OLD RICH MAN: Congratulations, here is all my money.

Ouija board

Oh, thank God ... Five young conjurers are trying to communicate with me. Now I can finally reveal the identity of my killer!

Is there a spirit present?

Yes!

(Giggling.)

Girls, listen to me. My name is Craig Swieskowski. I was murdered by a man named Bruce Kobza.

Does Trevor like Janet?

What? How should I know? Listen, Bruce Kobza poisoned me to death! There's a video recording of the murder in a locked briefcase in his apartment. You need to break into his bedroom, unlock the briefcase and show the tape to the police!

Y ... E ... S! (Hysterical laughter.) Trevor likes you, Janet!

Okay ... that's ... that's fine. I'm glad we got that out of our system. But now it's time to get serious. We might not have another chance to talk like this. I need you girls to go to Mt. Sinai Cemetery and dig up my body. Do an autopsy. You'll find—

Who likes Sophie?

Jesus, it's like you're not even listening to me! Bruce Kobza murdered me! *(sighing)* Okay ... fine, I'll try to use the damn board. B ...

B!

R...

R! Hey, he's spelling out Brian Pasternak! Brian Pasternak likes Sophie!

No!

Spirit? Are we pretty? Or ... do we need to lose a little bit of weight?

You don't need to lose any weight ... You should all be thankful you're alive and healthy.

L-O-S-E W-E-I-G-H-T. Guess we'll have to keep dieting, huh?

What? That's not what I said at all! *(Sighs.)* It doesn't matter.

Rebellion

Unfortunately, I started rebelling against my parents at around the same time I developed body odour.

– Son, I strongly suggest that you start wearing deodorant.
– Fuck you, Dad. I've got bigger plans.
– Please, son, I'm not the only one who feels strongly about this. Your teachers sent me a letter by messenger. It was signed by some of your classmates.
– Give the Man whatever he wants, right, Dad? Always obey the Man. That's your great philosophy of life.
– Yes, that's fine, son. Listen. It's really bad. The smell is really bad.
– Hey, Dad, guess what? I'm not going to synagogue anymore.
– Okay ... Please, son, I bought you these different kinds of deodorant. If you don't like any of them, I'll go back to the store and buy you more kinds. Hey, here's a cool one. It's for athletes.
– I'm moving out! I'm going to live under the overpass! Some of those people fought in *wars,* Dad. You didn't fight in any wars.
– Okay, that's ... All that's fine. Please put this on, son. You ... you carry my name.

Bar mitzvah

After you have your bar mitzvah, you will be a man in the eyes of God.

– my rabbi

June 7, 1997

GOD: Any bar mitzvahs today?
ANGEL: Yes ... Simon Rich has prepared twelve lines of Torah for his congregation at Central Synagogue.
GOD: Ah, then he must be *very* manly!
ANGEL: *(hesitating)* Yes.
GOD: Has this man started a family?
ANGEL: Um ... not yet.
GOD: I assume, though, that he has prospects?
ANGEL: I'm not sure I know how to answer that question.
GOD: I'd like to have a look at this strapping fellow! Where is he?
ANGEL: In his bedroom. *(Points.)*
GOD: Oh. Well ... I must admit he's not as robust as I would have imagined, given his mastery of Torah. But appearances aren't everything! What's that he's doing?
ANGEL: I believe he's playing a video game, sir. *Shufflepuck.*
GOD: Does it ... have to do with Torah?
ANGEL: Well, actually, it's sort of like air hockey. Except ... you play against space aliens, on a computer.
GOD: Why is he dancing?
ANGEL: I believe he just beat a challenging level.
GOD: So this dance is a kind of ... celebration.
ANGEL: Yes.
GOD: I take it from his enthusiasm that this is the first time he's beaten this particular level.
ANGEL: Well, actually, he does this dance whenever he beats *any* level of *any* video game. See ... there. He's doing it again.

GOD: Yes, I see. It's the same dance, all right.
ANGEL: It's usually not as ... frenetic ... as this. He's probably nervous about his upcoming bar mitzvah.
GOD: Who is that man, on the poster above his bed?
ANGEL: His name is Weird Al Yankovic.
GOD: I've never heard of him. Is he ... a Talmudic scholar?
ANGEL: Um ... *yes.*

A fantasy I had in seventh grade

Dear seventh graders,
Congratulations to all of the students who passed the Presidential Fitness Test! In three weeks, you will be engaged in warfare with the enemies of the United States.

I'd like to give special kudos to football co-captains Lance and Trevor, who both scored above the 90th percentile. You'll be going directly to the front lines.

Unfortunately, those of you who scored beneath the 35th percentile will not be allowed to participate in this war. You will, however, get to help out with strategizing – i.e., deciding which soldiers go on the most dangerous missions.

Also, I have been informed that while some of you lack athletic ability, you are very talented at computer simulation games. I cannot tell you how highly these skills are prized in today's modern army. Next week, we will be having a Presidential Videogame Fitness Test. Anyone who scores higher than 7,000 points on Crystal Quest will be given control of the entire Western Front. Anyone who scores higher than 8,000 points will become President.

Good luck to you all,
The President

Pen pal

In seventh grade, everyone in my class was assigned a foreign pen pal. Mine was from Bulgaria, and his name was Bojidar. We exchanged letters once a month, and at the end of the year we wrote reports about each other's countries based on what we had learned. Here is his report:

Life in the USA

By Bojidar

Of all the boys in the United States, Simon is the most popular. Simon is especially very popular with the girls at his school. I am very lucky that I was assigned the pen pal Simon, because it turns out that he is a very important American!

To the American girls, Simon is like a matador. They carry around in their pockets pictures of his face, and they trade the pictures to each other like they are currency. Rebecca, the most beautiful girl in America, wants to be his girlfriend but she does not say anything to him about it because she is afraid he will say no. The girls are impressed with Simon because (i) he does very well at all the videogames, and (2) he knows all the facts about the planets in outer space.

The cool things to wear in America are sweatpants, hand-me-down T-shirts, and big braces on your mouth and head. Another cool thing is to wear Velcro shoes. Here is a photograph of my pen pal. The average height for a thirteen-year-old boy in the United States is four feet five inches tall. So although he is small by the Bulgarian standard, in the United States, Simon is a boy of average size.

In the United States, a normal thing for boys is to go to a speech doctor every day after school to learn how to make the *l, s, r,* and *t* sounds. This is not something that is weird in the United States. In the United States, a cool thing is to listen to songs from the Disney movies, such as *Aladdin, Small Mermaid,* and *Beauty and the Beast.* Here is an example about that: One time my pen pal was listening to a tape of Disney songs on a Walkman machine, and Trevor, the leader of the lacrosse team, opened the machine and saw that the tape inside was *Small Mermaid.* There were a lot of girls from the school standing near them also. When Trevor looked at the tape, he said something like "That is a normal thing for a boy to be listening to, you are a cool guy." Then Trevor and the girls came over to Simon's house and they all listened to the Disney songs together and became friends. That is how things work in America.

If life were like middle school

JUDGE: In all my years on the bench, I have never seen a more despicable criminal. You robbed, assaulted, and tortured the victim simply for the thrill of it. Do you have anything to say in your defense before I sentence you?
CRIMINAL: Nope.
JUDGE: In that case, I hereby sentence you to forty years in a maximum security prison. I also sentence the victim to forty years in prison.
VICTIM: Wait – *what*? That doesn't make any sense! *He* attacked *me*!
JUDGE: I don't care who started it.

Ninth-grade experiments

1

OBSERVATION: None of the girls in my class think that I'm cool.

RESEARCH: My older brother told me that the political hard-core band Rage Against the Machine is cool.

HYPOTHESIS: If I pretend to be really into the political hard-core band Rage Against the Machine, then the girls in my class will think that I'm cool.

MATERIALS:

1 Rage Against the Machine album
1 Rage Against the Machine T-shirt
1 Rage Against the Machine bandanna

METHODS:

1) Wear the T-shirt and bandanna every single day for an entire month.
2) Make fun of everybody in the class for listening to bands that are less politically intense than Rage Against the Machine. Especially make fun of the girls who I am trying to impress.
3) Quote Rage Against the Machine lyrics constantly, regardless of the situation.
4) If someone asks me what I'm talking about, roll my eyes and say, "You probably wouldn't get it. It has to do with communism."
5) If someone calls my bluff and asks me what communism is, bang my fist against the table and say, *"God,* stop being such *a poser*!"

WAS YOUR HYPOTHESIS CORRECT? No.

2

OBSERVATION: None of the girls in my class think that I'm cool.

RESEARCH: Mike Cobalt wears gel in his hair and the girls think he's cool.

HYPOTHESIS: If I wear gel in my hair, then the girls will think I'm cool.

MATERIAL:
1 large bottle of Dep Shaping Gel (Extra Super Hold)

METHODS:

1) Wear gel in my hair every day for a week.
2) When my mom stops me at the elevator every morning and begs to help me use the gel because I "don't understand how it works," become so furious with her that I'm almost at the brink of tears.

WAS YOUR HYPOTHESIS CORRECT? No.

3

OBSERVATION: None of the girls in my class think that I'm cool. But one of the girls in my history class has started being nice to me.

RESEARCH: Sometimes when I'm eating lunch alone in the cafeteria, she sits down next to me, voluntarily. One time, when the two of us were alone in an elevator, she said, "God, Saturdays are so boring. I wish someone would take me to a movie or something."

HYPOTHESIS: If I ask her out, she might say yes – as long as I do it in a super-slick way.

MATERIALS:
3 cans of Jolt cola

METHODS:

1) Go to the bathroom at lunch and drink all three cans of Jolt to "get pumped."
2) Walk around her table in a circle until she motions for me to sit down next to her.
3) Pretend that I just noticed for the first time that she was sitting in the cafeteria, even though it's basically empty except for me and her.
4) Sit down across from her.
5) When she asks me if everything is okay, because parts of my face are twitching, tell her that I'm fine.
6) Don't say anything for ten whole minutes.
7) Tell her that *The Waterboy* starring Adam Sandler is opening on Friday.
8) Wait a little while for that information to sink in.
9) When she asks me if I'm planning on seeing it, say yes.
10) When she asks me if I'm going to see it with anyone, say no.
11) Stare at my tray for a few minutes, until she pokes me on the shoulder and says, "Hey ... do you want to ask me to go with you?"
12) Look up and nod.

WAS YOUR HYPOTHESIS CORRECT? Yes!

What I imagined the people around me were saying when I was …

Eleven

– Oh, man, I can't believe that kid Simon missed that ground ball! How pathetic!
– Wait … he's staring at his baseball glove with a confused expression on his face. Maybe there's something wrong with his glove and *that's* why he messed up?
– Yes, that's probably what happened.

Twelve

– Did that kid sitting behind us on the bus just get an erection?
– I don't know. For a while, I thought that was the case, but now that he's holding a book on his lap, it's impossible to tell.
– I guess we'll never know what the situation was.

Thirteen

– Hey, look, that thirteen-year-old is walking around with his mom!
– Where?
– There – in front of the supermarket!
– Oh my God! That kid is *way* too old to be hanging out with his mom. Even though I've never met him, I can tell he's a complete loser.
– Wait a minute … he's scowling at her and rolling his eyes.
– Oh, yeah … and I think I just heard him curse at her, for no reason.
– I guess he's cool after all.

Fourteen

– Why does that kid have a black X on the back of his right hand?
– I bet it's because he went to some kind of cool rock concert last night.
– Wow … he must've stayed out pretty late if he didn't have time to scrub it off.

– Yeah, and that's probably why his hair is so messy and unwashed. Because he cares more about rocking out than conforming to society.
– Even though he isn't popular in the traditional sense, I respect him from afar.

Fifteen

– Hey, look, that kid is reading *Howl* by Allen Ginsberg.
– Wow. He must be some kind of rebel genius.
– I'm impressed by the fact that he isn't trying to call attention to himself.
– Yeah, he's just sitting silently in the corner, flipping the pages and nodding, with total comprehension.
– It's amazing: he's so absorbed in his book that he isn't even aware that a party is going on around him, with dancing and fun.
– Why aren't any girls going over and talking to him?
– I guess they're probably a little intimidated by his brilliance.
– Well, who *wouldn't* be?
– I'm sure the girls will talk to him soon.
– It's only a matter of time.

Sixteen

– Hey, look, it's that kid Simon who wrote that scathing poem for the literary magazine.
– You mean the one about how people are phonies? Wow – I loved that poem!
– Me too. Reading it made me realize for the first time that everyone is a phony, including me.
– The only person at this school who isn't a phony is Simon.
– Yeah. He sees right through us.

My friend's new girlfriend

My friend Jared found a girlfriend this summer, and I am *so* jealous. We're the two least popular kids in the ninth grade and we've always been best friends. But now Jared's always bragging about his girlfriend and how awesome she is. It makes me feel so pathetic. I've never had a girlfriend before, but this girl sounds incredible. Her name is Tiffany Sparkle. She goes to a different school, a modelling academy in New Brunswick. He showed me some pictures of her from magazines, and believe me, she is *hot*. He met her over the summer, when he was visiting his grandparents in Canada. He saved her life. She was about to get run over by a double-decker bus when all of a sudden Jared skateboarded through traffic and pushed her out of the way. There was a huge crowd of Canadians standing around, and when Jared saved Tiffany's life everybody just started cheering like crazy. Then she kissed him on the mouth. When I heard that story, I was like "Give me a break!" because it was just about the coolest thing I had ever heard in my entire life! They spent the rest of the summer having sex all over the place in all of the different sex positions. And now they talk every night on the phone.

The amazing thing about this girl is that she isn't just hot. She also shares a lot of Jared's interests. She's totally into Web design and the game Warcraft. And she's also really shy. For example, when she visited Jared over spring break, she didn't want to meet me because she was too embarrassed. When I heard that, I was like "Come on!" because that is *so* like Jared. It's kind of amazing that they found each other.

There are other similarities too. Like, he showed me a letter she wrote him last week about how she wanted to try out some new kind of sex position, and at first I thought he had written it *himself* because their handwritings are *so* similar. Tiffany also has severe bronchial asthma, which is pretty great for Jared, because now he has someone to talk to about that.

The big ninth grade dance is in four days. I asked Jared to set me up with one of Tiffany's friends from her modelling academy, but he said that everybody there already has a boyfriend. I asked him for advice on how to find a date, but all of his suggestions involved saving girls' lives. In the end, I decided to just walk up to this girl I like named Laura and ask her point-blank if she wanted to go with me. I was so nervous that my arms and legs were shaking really fast like they do in gym class when the teacher says it's my turn to lead stretches. But I asked her anyway and she said yes.

I talk to Laura on the phone every night now, which is pretty great, because Jared never has time to talk to me anymore. *He's* not even going to the dance! Tiffany's flying to the U.S. for one night only and she hates dancing so they're just going to stay home and try out new sex positions. It's amazing. I mean, don't get me wrong. My date Laura is pretty cool, and other than her leg brace she's very attractive, but she's certainly no Canadian model. It's hard to believe that when I'm on the dance floor this Friday, trying to work up the guts to kiss Laura for the first time, Jared's going to be at home in his bedroom making love to the girl of his dreams. Some guys have all the luck.

Animals

Free-range chickens

– Well, it's another beautiful day in paradise.
– How'd we get so lucky?
– I don't know and I don't care.
– I think I'll go walk over there for a while. Then I'll walk back here.
– That sounds like a good time. Maybe I'll do the same.
– Hey, someone refilled the grain bucket!
– Is it the same stuff as yesterday?
– I hope so.
– Oh, man ... it's the same stuff all right.
– It's *so good.*
– I can't stop eating it.
– Hey, you know what would go perfectly with this grain? Water.
– Dude. Look inside the other bucket.
– This ... is the greatest day of my life.
– Drink up, pal.
– Cheers!
(Laughs.)
(Laughs.)
– Hey, look, the farmer's coming.
– Huh. Guess its my turn to go into the thing.
– Cool. See you later, buddy.
– See ya.

Dalmatians

– Hey, look, the truck's stopping.
– Did they take us to the park this time?
– No ... it's a fire. Another horrible fire.
– What the hell is wrong with these people?

Herbert Hoover

HERBERT HOOVER: If I'm elected president, I promise that there will be a car in every garage and a chicken in every pot.
FIRST CHICKEN: Jesus Christ, did you guys hear that?
SECOND CHICKEN: Hear what?
FIRST CHICKEN: Some guy running for president just said on the radio that he was going to kill one chicken per U.S. family!
SECOND CHICKEN: Seriously? He singled us out?
FIRST CHICKEN: *Yes.* It was like some kind of crazy vow.
SECOND CHICKEN: What are we going to do?

Prehistoric life

Prehistoric camping

– Hey, man, do you want to go camping this weekend?
– What do you mean?
– I was thinking we could climb a mountain and, you know, hang out for a couple of days.
– Why?
– I don't know ... I just sort of feel like getting away for a while.
– Getting away from what? Are there any predators coming?
– No.
– *Did you see any predators?*

Prehistoric small talk

– Hey, Ted. Seen any predators?
– Nope. You?
– Nah. Not lately.
– What are you up to this weekend?
– I don't know. I'll probably stand on a rock, look out for predators.
– Yeah. Same here.

Prehistoric marriage

– Do you take this woman to be your lawful wedded wife?
– I do.
– Have you seen any predators?
– No.
– Has *anyone* seen any predators?
(pause)
– Okay ... we're safe for a little while.

The dog X-files

Here are some scenes for a TV show I came up with that's exactly like *The X-Files* except all of the characters are dogs.

REX: Thank God you're here. I didn't know who else to turn to. No one believes my story.
DOG SCULLY: Tell us what happened.
REX: I used to go into the living room every day. I'd run around, scratch up the couches – you know, have a good time. Then yesterday, I went inside and all of a sudden a horrible electric shock shot through my entire body.
DOG MULDER: Unbelievable.
DOG SCULLY: Did you try going in again today?
REX: Yes. The same thing happened. I don't even want to go into that room anymore.
DOG MULDER: Wow. I have no explanation.

DOG MULDER: I'm Agent Mulder from the Dog FBI. Tell us what happened.
SKIP: Last week, my face was really itchy. I kept trying to scratch my nose, but ... I couldn't reach it.
DOG MULDER: What do you mean?
SKIP: There was some kind of cone-shaped force field surrounding my head.
DOG SCULLY: Incredible!
SKIP: The crazy thing is, three days later, I fell asleep ... and when I woke up, the force field was gone.
DOG SCULLY: I don't understand. This defies all logic!
DOG MULDER: Not everything can be explained with logic, Dog Scully.

BOOMER: This is really hard for me. You're the first people I've told.

DOG SCULLY: Tell us what happened. Maybe we can help.
BOOMER: Okay, here goes. Yesterday I fell asleep, and when I woke up, my testicles were missing.
DOG SCULLY: Jesus. This is the fifth case this month.
DOG MULDER: There's something happening out there. Something beyond our understanding.

ROCKET: I used to have fleas all over my body. Thousands and thousands of them. Then, yesterday, I felt a tightness around my neck ... and within hours the fleas were gone.
DOG MULDER: (Spits out coffee.)
DOG SCULLY: For years, I've tried to be a scientist, to live by the rules of logic and reason. But now I don't know what to believe.
DOG MULDER: Please use your magic to kill my fleas.

Animal cruelty

In order to learn more about animal cruelty, I built a translating machine and interviewed several farm animals about their current situation.

Cow

– You've been incarcerated in this slaughterhouse your entire life. How has it affected you emotionally?
– I am cow. I eat grass. Grass on ground. Me move mouth down to grass. Chew up grass.
– Do you think animal slavery will end in your lifetime?
– Eat grass, rest. Eat grass, rest. Sleep.
– Do you feel that animals deserve the same rights as human beings?
– Grass on ground. Eat it all up.

Chicken

– You've lived inside this 26- × 22-inch cage your entire life. How does it feel to know that you will never meet your family?
– Food in bag. Eat it up.
– Are "free range" chickens truly free? Or do they suffer the same indignities as standard, factory-produced chickens?
– Me eat food in bag. Rest. Sleep.

Pig

– Human beings have mistreated your species for centuries, caging you in tiny prisons and pumping you full of dangerous hormones, just to make money. If you could say one thing to your human oppressors, what would it be?
– Give me more of the things that go inside my mouth. I like the things that I put inside my mouth. Chew it all up good. Rest, sleep.
– I understand that your owner castrated you at birth and then branded you with a fiery hot iron. Does it ever get so bad that you wish for death?
– Give me more of the things that go inside my mouth.

Lost puppy!

Our beloved family pet is missing! We lost him on *this block* and he probably hasn't gone far. If you find a dog that matches the following description, please give me a call!

Thanks!
– Suzie

Large claws

Extra set of teeth

Red eyes

Quick to anger

Often unreasonable; lacks the self-control of other dogs

Likes to stand on his hind legs and rise to his full height so he can look people in the eye

Often stays in shadowy areas; very hard to spot sometimes, except for his eyes, which always have a faint red glow

Fast

When he stands on his hind legs and looks people in the eye, he expects them to maintain eye contact; if they look away even for a second, he has a kind of breakdown

If he's having a rampage and someone escapes, he likes to come find them, usually on the one-year anniversary of the rampage

Answers to the name "Ctharga," but if his name is said three times, something weird happens to his eyes and he somehow becomes even faster than he is normally

Silent

Ant farm

– All right men, listen up. As you know, we've built seven tunnels and we still haven't found a way through the glass. I can tell you're discouraged and I don't blame you. Tunnel 7 was our most ambitious project to date and you all risked your lives to make it happen. But rest assured, we'll be out of this hellish wasteland soon enough. I have a plan.
– What is it? What's the plan?
– An eighth tunnel. Through the sand.
– I don't know, sir ... we've been digging tunnels ever since we got here. We always end up hitting glass. We lost ten men on the last tunnel: Brian, Jack, Lawrence—
– I know their names.
– Why don't we just give up? I mean seriously, what's the point?
– The point? The point is we have no food or water. The point is we're trapped in this crazy desert, and if we don't find an exit soon we're going to suffocate.
– What kind of God would put us here, just to torture us? Sand to the left ... sand to the right ...
– It's a test, William. He's testing us.
– You're right. We can do this. We just have to work ten times harder than we've ever worked before! (Starts digging.)
– You want to know something? I've got a good feeling about this one. A really good feeling.

Going to work

Great astronaut quotes throughout history

"That's one small step for man, one giant leap for mankind."

– Neil Armstrong, 1969

"Orbiting Earth, I see how beautiful our planet is. Let us preserve and increase this beauty, not destroy it."

– Yuri Gagarin, 1961

"What's happening? Where am I?"

– Ham the Chimp, 1960

Employees must wash hands

Employees must wash hands before returning to work, including Ivan.

Ivan must wash his *entire* hands: palms, thumbs and in particular his fingers.

Ivan must not do that thing he often does where he runs the water for a few seconds, to make it sound like he's washing his hands, but doesn't actually wash his hands. He must *really* wash his hands – both of them – using soap.

When Ivan is hand-mixing the sauces, he mustn't do that thing he thinks is so funny where he winks at the other chefs to imply that he hasn't actually washed his hands. He should just wash his hands and then go mix the sauces. That's his job. He should just do his job. It's not that hard to wash your hands.

Employees must take their medication before returning to work to suppress the contagious flare-ups on their hands. This rule is directed primarily at Ivan.

Notices for tonight's magic show

Please note that in Hector the Amazing's final trick – "The Sawing of Susan" – the role of "Susan" will be played by Alice Jenkins. Alice is replacing Patricia Merkle, who is replacing Joan Greenblatt, who is replacing Jenny Holden who is replacing Susan Bender who is replacing Jenna Hertle who is replacing Tanya Lintle who originated the role seven performances ago.

We are also looking for contributions to the legal fund of Hector the Amazing. Hector, as you may have read, has been accused (unjustly!) of over half-a-dozen heinous crimes against women. We are confident that he will beat these charges which are completely baseless. There is no hard evidence that Hector was even present at the scene of these atrocities – no photographs, no video, no audio recordings.

We ask that you refrain from taking photographs, video or audio recordings during tonight's magic show.

Please note that if you are attending tonight's *second* performance, the role of Susan will not be played by Alice Jenkins, but by another woman, as yet to be determined. If you are attending tonight's third performance, Susan will be played by still another woman.

Portions of tonight's show may be inappropriate for children under the age of 18.

Enjoy the show.

Physician's Lounge

– You wanted to see me, sir?
– Yes, Dr. Metzger. I'm afraid I've got some bad news. I've been receiving complaints from your patients. And I've decided I can't allow you to make April Fools jokes this year.
– Oh my God.
– I know you're disappointed, but my mind is made up.
– What about the one where I tell the patient I'm out of anesthetic?
– No.
– What about the one where I put on a janitor's outfit, grab a scalpel and walk into the operating room just as my patient loses consciousness? So he thinks he's going to be operated on by a janitor?
– No.
– What about the one where the patient wakes up after his operation and I start shouting, "Where's my stethoscope? Where did I leave my stethoscope?" And then I stare at the patient's torso, with a look of horror, like I maybe left it inside of his body?
– No.
– You can't do this to me! April Fools Day is the highlight of my year. It's the only reason I finished medical school – to experience the holiday as a doctor.
– I'm sorry, Sam, but my hands are tied.
– What about the one where the patient wakes up and I'm wearing a robot costume, so he thinks he's been in a coma for eighty years. And I'm, like, "Welcome to the future, Mr. Greenbaum, the world you remember is gone." You know, in a robot voice. So he thinks I'm a robot.
– I get it. The answer is still no.
– How could you be so cruel? I mean, for God's sake, what happened to the Hippocratic Oath?
– "First do no harm?"

– That's what that meant?
– Yes.
– You sure?
– Yes.
– It wasn't something about April Fools?
– No.
– What about the one where I tell the patient his kidney operation was a grand success, but then, while I'm talking to him, I have an intern come in and say, "Dr. Metzger, you've got some dirt on your left shoulder." And I start to brush my right shoulder. And the intern's like, "no, your left shoulder." And I'm like, "this *is* my left shoulder." And he's like, "No, it's your right shoulder. What's the matter with you, Dr. Metzger? Don't you know your left from your right?" And then we both look at the patient's torso, with a look of horror, to imply, like ...
– I know where you're going with this.
– ... to imply, like, maybe I operated on the wrong kidney? Like, maybe I did the left one, instead of the right one. Because I don't know the difference between right and left.
– No.
– At least let me workshop it!
– I'm sorry, Sam, but my decision is final.
– ...
– April ... Fools.
– NO WAY!
– I can't believe you bought that.
– *Man*, you got me good. Guess that's why you're the head of surgery.
– Pass me my robot mask. It's time to make the rounds.

Swim at your own risk

– There is no life guard on duty after 9pm

– The life guard on duty before 9pm is a 16-year-old boy

– The 16-year-old boy is an open marijuana user. He has vowed to spend the summer "always high." He smokes pot the moment he wakes up, which means that by the time he sits down in his lifeguard chair, at 9am, he is already high.

– The life guard is on break from noon to 1pm. It is during this time that he goes from "high" to "stoned."

– The life guard's high peaks at around 4pm. By this point in the day, the boy is so narcotized, he actually loses contact with reality. His brain stops fighting the drugs and instead "gives in" to their effects. Rational thought ceases and his world becomes a dream-like wash of shapes and colors.

– From 5–9pm there is a second life guard on duty. She is a 15-year-old girl. She uses less marijuana than the boy, but still enough to be classified, by any rubric, as a full-fledged drug addict. The boy and the girl are beginning to fall in love. They spend the afternoons having earnest conversations about life's great mysteries. One common discussion topic is how the world "might be a dream," in which case "nothing matters." They never look out at the water, only into each other's eyes, two carefree children, high beyond reason, living only for today.

– The water contains sharks.

Choose your own adventure

In Choose Your Own Adventure 17 you were a prince of England, *jousting your way to the throne! In Choose Your Own Adventure 46 you were a* boy rock star, *jamming your way up the charts! Now, in Choose Your Own Adventure 92, you're a* grown-up, *working as a Corporate Software Designer in Poughkeepsie.*

Page one

You wake up at 7:45. The alarm clock never went off, but it doesn't matter. You've gotten so used to waking up every single day at the same time that it just happens automatically now. You feel so horrible you can barely even believe it. Suddenly you remember that it's Wednesday. That means there's going to be one of those Projects Meetings and you're going to have to sit through the entire three-hour nightmare as soon as you get to work. Maybe you should just call in sick? You have three sick days and you've only used one so far. Then again, if you use your second sick day now, you'll only have one left.

If you decide to use your sick day now, turn to Page Two. If you decide to save your sick day for some other time, turn to Page Six.

Page two

You call the office and tell them you're sick.

"That's your second sick day," Nancy tells you. "You only have one left."

"I know," you say, hanging up the phone.

How did this happen? How did this become your life?

You try to go back to sleep, but it's impossible. After about five minutes, you sit up and turn on the television. That's when you remember: the cable in your apartment is broken and the guy isn't coming to fix it until Saturday. You flip around for a while, but the only channels you get are CBS and NBC. CBS is playing *The Early Show*. NBC is playing the *Today* show.

If you decide to watch The Early Show *on CBS, turn to Page Three.*
If you decide to watch the Today *show on NBC, turn to Page Four.*

Page three

You watch *The Early Show. Turn to Page Five.*

Page four

You watch the *Today* show. *Turn to Page Five.*

Page five

You go to the bathroom and look at your face. What happened? You used to be young and it wasn't so long ago. Jesus. Maybe you should have just gone to work.

THE END

Page six

You go to work. The Projects Meeting is about as horrible as you expected. It's just the same thing every time. Mr. Cohen talking about "viability," and everybody nodding and looking at the clock, waiting for lunch to start, like a bunch of animals. When you get down to it, everybody is basically just an animal – eating, sleeping, eating, sleeping. Dying. Christ. Maybe you should have just called in sick.

THE END

Actor's nightmare

Ford's theater, 1865

*(*LADY HAMPTON *and* LORD HAMPTON *enter stage right.)*

LADY HAMPTON: Good afternoon, sir.

LORD HAMPTON: Good afternoon.

(President Lincoln shot in the head.)

STAGE MANAGER: *(offstage)* Keep going!

Demands

Dear cops,
I'll release the hostages if you bring me the following items:

1) Combination to bank vault or some kind of machine that can open vaults
2) A strong bag that is big enough to fit all of the money from the vault
3) A second criminal to help me carry this bag out of the bank
4) Ropes to tie up the hostages so they don't walk around so much
5) A third criminal with a car who can drive us away as soon as we get outside with the bag
6) MapQuest directions from the bank parking lot to Mexico
7) Some general information on Mexico (what kind of currency they use, which sports are popular there, basic culture things)
8) English to Spanish dictionary
9) Someone needs to go back to my apartment and bring me my asthma inhaler. It's either in the medicine cabinet or on the little table next to the futon.
10) There's a small chance I left the stove on in my apartment. I don't think I did, but I'm a little bit worried because I can't actually visualize myself turning it off. Anyway, whichever policeman goes to get the inhaler should also check to make sure the burner is all the way off because I left my cat behind and I don't want him to inhale any gas.
11) I just realized that someone is going to have to adopt my cat. His name is Rudy and he is very smart and affectionate. I'm not just saying that because he is mine – he is a really special animal. He has a slight bladder problem but it's not bad as long as you give him his medication (the directions are on the bottle).

12) I forgot to give Rudy his pill this morning. Just give him two tonight. You're really not supposed to do it like that, but it's okay if it ends up happening once in a while.
13) Some kind of weapon.

Gotham City Hall

BATMAN: Thanks for taking the time to meet with me, Mayor.
MAYOR: Of course, Batman. What's on your mind?
BATMAN: It's about the prison system. I really think you should increase funding.
MAYOR: We've already been over this, Batman. We simply don't have the resources.
BATMAN: But Gotham City *needs* a maximum security prison. I mean ... look at these statistics. *(Takes out pie chart.)* Scarecrow has escaped eleven times. The Riddler has escaped sixty-four times. The Joker has escaped *four thousand times.* It's like, what's the point of even *having* a prison?
MAYOR: I wish there was something I could do, but the annual budget's already been finalized.
BATMAN: You know these guys are trying to kill me, right?
MAYOR: I'll tell you what: I can transfer the Joker to the Asylum for the Criminally Insane. That's a secure location.
BATMAN: Are you kidding me? That place is a freaking *joke*!
MAYOR: ...
BATMAN: I'm sorry ... I was out of line.
MAYOR: That's all right. I know this is an emotional issue for you.
BATMAN: I just don't have any confidence in that asylum. Last month they released the Penguin and *three days later* he tried to kill me. I was able to capture him and have him recommitted to the asylum, but they released him again the very next day! He tried to kill me this morning. I barely escaped. He's still on the loose.
MAYOR: Believe me, Batman, I sympathize.
BATMAN: Listen. I've been crunching the numbers, and if we eliminate the Gotham Symphony Orchestra, we can hire four extra guards and build a watchtower.

MAYOR: Batman, the orchestra is one of the jewels of our city.
BATMAN: I know, I know ... but don't you think we've reached a crisis situation?
MAYOR: It's just ... less costly to keep things the way they are. And besides, you can handle these guys! You're *Batman.* You don't need some fancy, expensive new prison.
BATMAN: Is that new? That flat screen TV?
MAYOR: ...
(Phone rings.)
MAYOR: Excuse me, Batman. *(Picks up phone.)* Mayor Hayes here ... really? Kidnapped? What did the note say? Huh ... it sounds like some kind of *riddle.* Nah, don't worry about the signal. He's right here. *(Hangs up.)* It seems the governor's daughter has been kidnapped.
BATMAN: Again? That's the third time this month!
MAYOR: It sounds like the work of the Riddler. Apparently he's ... um ... escaped from prison.
BATMAN: ...
MAYOR: Hey, at least you're already dressed, right? I mean, that saves us a call on the red phone.
BATMAN: You know what my red phone bill was last month? Eleven hundred dollars. That money comes straight out of my own pocket.
MAYOR: Do you want a key to the city?
BATMAN: I already have seventy-four keys to the city. I don't need another key to the damn city. All I want is some accountability here.
MAYOR: I'll tell you what: I'll talk to that philanthropist, Bruce Wayne. I bet I can convince him to donate us a prison. That guy's a real pushover.
BATMAN: ...
MAYOR: You know there's a rumour going around that he had a facelift?
BATMAN: Really? Who's been saying that?
MAYOR: *(Shrugs.)* Everybody.

World's oldest profession

If prostitution really is the "world's oldest profession," that means there was a time when it was the only job on earth.

20,000 B.C.

MAN: Hey.
WOMAN: Hey.
MAN AND WOMAN: *(in unison)* You want some action?
MAN: Damn. Thought I had a sale.
WOMAN: Me too.
MAN: Hey, do you mind if I go after the next customer? It's been a really slow week for me.
WOMAN: Go ahead.
MAN: Thanks. Hello, sir!
SECOND MAN: Want some action?
MAN: *(Sighs.)*
SECOND MAN: *(to woman)* Want some action?

19,000 B.C.

MAN: Guess what? I came up with a new profession. It's called "carpenter."
WOMAN: Is it sort of like "prostitute"?
MAN: No, it's a totally different thing. I make things out of wood and sell them to other people.
WOMAN: Sell them? For what?
MAN: Sex, usually. I mean ... my customers are all prostitutes.
WOMAN: Oh. Want some action?
MAN: Do *you* want some action?
WOMAN: I thought you said you were a carpenter now.
MAN: I'm not quitting my day job.

Worst nightmare

POLICE OFFICER: Mr. Rich? We need to speak to you.
ME: Is there a problem, Officer?
SECOND POLICE OFFICER: Your neighbour Mrs. Hamilton was murdered today, and you match the witness's description. I'd call that a problem.
ME: Officer, I swear, I had nothing to do with it!
SECOND POLICE OFFICER: We'll need an alibi. Where were you this afternoon?
ME: At what time?
SECOND POLICE OFFICER: From eight A.M. to six P.M.
ME: I was here. In my apartment.
POLICE OFFICER: Really? On a Wednesday?
SECOND POLICE OFFICER: Why weren't you at work?
ME: Well, I'm a writer, so I work from home.
POLICE OFFICER: So you were writing. What were you working on?
SECOND POLICE OFFICER: I don't see any writing materials around.
ME: Well ... actually ... I didn't really get much work done today.
POLICE OFFICER: So what did you *do* all day?
ME: I watched TV.
POLICE OFFICER: For the entire day?
ME: Um ... yeah.
POLICE OFFICER: What did you watch?
ME: Does it really matter?
POLICE OFFICER: Yes.
ME: Okay ... I watched *Nanny 911*.
POLICE OFFICER: What's that?
ME: It's a reality show about a group of British nannies. They visit American households and try to get them to be more organized.
SECOND POLICE OFFICER: What else?
ME: That's it. Just ... that one show.
POLICE OFFICER: You watched *Nanny 911* for ten straight hours?

ME: There was a marathon.
SECOND POLICE OFFICER: Jesus. What about meals?
ME: I ordered in pizza. Once at noon and then again at around five.
POLICE OFFICER: You ordered pizza twice in one day?
SECOND POLICE OFFICER: *(picking up copy of* TV Guide*)* Hey, it says here that the *Nanny 911* marathon was only five hours long. Your story doesn't hold up.
ME: Well ... the thing is ... they ran the marathon twice. Once from eight to one ... and then again, from one to six.
POLICE OFFICER: Wait a minute. You're telling us you watched five episodes of *Nanny 911,* from eight to one. And then you watched the same five episodes *again,* from one to six?
(long pause)
ME: I murdered Mr. Hamilton.
POLICE OFFICER: You mean *Mrs.* Hamilton?
ME: Whatever.

The only e-mails I could receive that would justify the frequency with which I check my e-mail

Hey Simon,
It's Danielle, the quiet girl you said "hi" to once at Academic Camp the summer after junior year of high school. I'd explain how I tracked you down and got your e-mail address, but there just isn't enough time: in three minutes, I'm leaving on a jet plane for the Bahamas. (I know – I should have e-mailed earlier!) Anyway, I've been secretly in love with you for the past six years and I want you to come live with me in paradise. If you write back in the next three minutes, I can get the pilot to wait for you. If you don't respond by then, I'll have no choice but to assume that our feelings are not reciprocal.

Danielle

Dear Mr. Rich,
This is the IRS. We have a feeling that you may have accidentally exaggerated some of your business expenses this year, but we don't want to trouble you with something as unpleasant as a tax audit. Can you do us a favour and just send over a quick e-mail confirming that you told the truth on all of your forms? You don't have to explain your specific expenses – you can just put "It's all true" in the subject heading, or something to that effect. If you write us back before the tax deadline, which is in three minutes, then we'll consider this matter closed. Otherwise, we'll have no choice but to take your silence as an admission of guilt and send you to prison.

IRS

Hey Simon,
How's it going? It's Craig from high school. I just wanted to say hey

and see what you were up to. I just started working for a company called Skylar Labs and it's been really exciting. In fact, I'm actually on my way to a press conference right now. In three minutes we're unveiling a really cool new product to the public. It's hard to explain, but basically it stops the spread of cancer cells while simultaneously giving patients the ability to fly. I wonder if the announcement will have any effect on our company's stock prices? Anyway, hope everything's cool with you and I'll talk to you later.

Craig

Dear Mr. Rich,
Three minutes ago, NASA confirmed that a moon-sized asteroid is on a collision course with Earth. In preparation for this day, the government has built an escape pod, called simply, "The Ark." You are among the ten humans who have been selected to board the pod and serve as the progenitors for a new race of men which will live on after our planet has exploded. The other humans going into the pod are Jack Nicholson, a brilliant scientist, and the seven most beautiful women on the planet. Please write us back in the next few minutes to confirm that you're willing to take part in this mission. If you're uncomfortable with this level of power and celebrity, just ignore this e-mail and in three minutes your seat will be given to someone else.

God bless you,
The President

An interview with Stephen Hawking

REPORTER: I just want to start off by saying what a huge fan I am.
STEPHEN HAWKING: Thank you so much.
REPORTER: How does it feel to know that your seminal work, *A Brief History of Time,* has sold over two million copies worldwide?
STEPHEN HAWKING: It's an incredible honour. I'm still shocked, to be honest, that it was published in the first place. It isn't very often that *I Love Lucy* fan fiction makes its way onto the shelves.
REPORTER: I'm sorry ... did you say "*I Love Lucy* fan fiction"?
STEPHEN HAWKING: Yes, that's what my book is: a series of stories that I wrote using the characters from *I Love Lucy.* They travel around the world together, having zany adventures.
REPORTER: I thought it was about astrophysics. Like ... black holes.
STEPHEN HAWKING: That's only the first three chapters. In the middle of chapter four the narrative spirals off into *I Love Lucy* fan fiction and stays there for the remainder of the book.
REPORTER: Really?
STEPHEN HAWKING: *Yes.* I must say, I'm pretty surprised you didn't notice. It's almost as if you started to read my book, got bored, and then quit after just a few pages.
REPORTER: ...
STEPHEN HAWKING: Oh my God. That's what happened, isn't it? You bought my book, because you wanted to look smart, but you never even read past page fifty! I'm right, aren't I?
REPORTER: I'm sorry, Dr. Hawking.
STEPHEN HAWKING: Has *anyone* finished my book?

The final moments of the *Titanic*

According to legend, the *Titanic* band continued to play music as their ship went down. They never abandoned their instruments or sought places in the lifeboats. Instead, they used their final moments to calm their fellow passengers with popular melodies and lovely waltzes.

CAPTAIN: You gentlemen are an inspiration, even to an old sea dog like me.
CELLIST: Thank you, sir.
CAPTAIN: While there's still time, I'd like to make one last request. Would you play "Nearer, My God, to Thee"? It's my favourite hymn.
VIOLINIST: Of course, sir. That's my favourite hymn too. A-one and a-two and a ... wait a minute ... what do you mean "last request"? I thought we were getting paid to play until six.
CELLIST: Yeah, our contract says "midnight to six."
CAPTAIN: Well, yes ... but I imagine the end will come by then. I mean, if the ship continues to sink at this rate.
VIOLIST: If the ship continues to *what! (Looks up from his sheet music.)* Holy *shit!* Guys, look!
DRUMMER: Jesus *Christ*! Is that a fucking *hole* in the *ship?*
CELLIST: Oh my God. Oh my God oh my God oh my God oh my God ...
CAPTAIN: I don't understand. Didn't you men hear the *collision*?
VIOLINIST: We couldn't hear anything over the sound of our instruments!
CAPTAIN: What about all the crowds of screaming people running by? You must've noticed them.
DRUMMER: I thought they were just excited because we were playing so many waltzes! Why didn't you tell us that the ship was *sinking?*
CAPTAIN: I assumed you knew and were playing anyway. You know, as a kind of ... gesture.

CELLIST: Are you *insane? (turning to his bandmates)* Guys, listen, I have a plan: the rule is usually women and children first, but if we *dress up as women,* then maybe we can sneak onto the lifeboats!
VIOLINIST: It'll never work! We all have *beards!*
DRUMMER: Maybe we can *kill* the women and children, to make more space!
CELLIST: *(nodding seriously)* I have a revolver in my room.
VIOLINIST: It's too late! The final lifeboat is leaving!
VIOLIST: *(sobbing)* What are we going to *do?*
CELLIST: Let's keep playing! Maybe if we do it loud and fast enough, one of the boats will hear us and come back!
DRUMMER: It's our only chance.

Inside the cartridge

Street Fighting Man, copyright © 1987 by Nintendo Scene: Jump Kick Boulevard

– How many dead?
– Fifty.
Christ. Exactly the same as yesterday. How's morale?
– Terrible. It's like we're not even trying out there. We don't stand a chance against ... well ... you know.
– (shuddering) He-Who-Is-Dressed-Differently.
– He's immortal, and I'll swear to that. Today he stopped in midstride and began to punch the air. Five of our brothers walked directly into his moving fist. One by one, they fell to the ground and vanished.
– There is no God.
– Every day he defeats us in the exact same sequence, using the exact same manoeuvres.
– And that music. It never stops!
– The same sixteen notes, over and over again, droning and endless, piercing through the darkened void. (hushed) Sometimes he brings a companion to help him with his murders.
– Their blows hurt us but not each other!
– It is as if God has chosen us alone for misery.
– (sobbing) Why does he rush through our town so quickly?
– I believe he's going for a record of some kind. It has to do with points.
– Sweet Lord!
– It's not enough for him to simply take our lives. He must also take our honour.
– You would think by now he would have grown tired of this battle. Surely the challenge is gone!
– And yet the genocide continues.

– Was it always like this, brother?
– I do not know.
– Hold me, brother, I'm frightened!
– (punches him in the face) I'm sorry. That seems to be the only action I'm capable of.
– I only have two hits left.

THE END

Role playing

TEACHER: All right, class, today we're going to be learning about the political landscape that led to the Civil War. Let's start with a little role-playing exercise. First we need someone to play the part of a Southern slave owner. Okay, let's say ... Seymour.
SEYMOUR: What?
TEACHER: Great. Now we need someone to play a Northern abolitionist. Raise your hand if you want to volunteer. Okay – I guess that's everybody else. Let's begin.
SOPHIE: How many innocent people must die to satisfy your greed, Seymour?
KAREN: You're a monster, Seymour. (crying) A *monster.*
SEYMOUR: What's happening? I'm against slavery – I swear!
TEACHER: I don't think that's something a slave owner would say, Seymour. Remember, you're being graded on this.
SEYMOUR: Um ... then, I guess ... slavery ... is good?
TEACHER: Of all the villains in the history of this nation, you, Seymour, are by far the most terrifying. I can't even look you in the face. You literally make my skin crawl.
SEYMOUR: I thought you said it was a role-playing exercise?
TEACHER: I'm also doing the exercise. I'm an abolitionist.

Crayola Co.

– Thanks for coming, Samuel.
– No problem, boss. I'll have those new colour names on your desk by five.
– That's fine. Listen, Sam ... have you been having problems at home?
– Well, actually, yeah. How did you know? Who told you?
– Well ... to be honest, I could sort of tell by the quality of your work.
– But I've been writing ten crayon titles a day!
– I know, but some of these colours ... Sad Blue ... Sad Green ... Horrible Red ... Sad Red ... Really Sad Blue ... Divorce Sienna ... Divorce Brown ... Divorce Green ... Divorce Pink ... It's just ... a little repetitive, you know?
– Well, all the colours have been more or less the same lately. What can I say? When it comes to crayon naming, you have to go with your first instinct. Like, look at this new shade of orange. What pops into your mind?
– I don't know ... sunshine?
– Well, yeah. Or divorce. I would say Divorce Orange. Except there already is a Divorce Orange. So then ... I guess, no name. Just a nameless colour.
– I think maybe you need a vacation.
– Really?
– Look, to be honest, last month's colours were a little off too. Adultery Red ... Ultimatum Pink ... Lawyers Green ... Settlement Blue ... Countersettlement Light Blue ... Maybe you need to take some time away from the office. You know, to resolve the crisis in your marriage?
– Look, boss. No offense, but I'm just not buying all this psychobabble. I mean, Craig came up with Ladybug Red today. That doesn't mean he has a bug problem at home or whatever.
– Okay. But what about your colours from *two* months ago?

Temptation Red? Considering Adultery Blue? Considering Adultery Yellow?
– What about them?
– I think you should take the rest of the day off.
– Okay, you're the boss. I guess I'll see you divorce.
– Do you mean ... "I'll see you tomorrow?"
– That's what I said.

How I imagine life in the U.S. army (based on the commercials I've seen)

GENERAL STONE: All right, men, listen up! Our nation is at war, and the whole world is counting on us to protect freedom. That leaves us with just one option.
BOB: Rock climbing?
GENERAL STONE: Exactly. There's a steep mountain in the middle of an unpopulated desert. We need someone to go there by himself, climb the mountain, and put a flag on the top.
BOB: I'll do it.
GENERAL STONE: Excellent! Here's the flag.
BOB: Cool.
GENERAL STONE: All right, let's see. We also need someone to ride a Jet Ski. How about you, Jackson?
JACKSON: I don't know, General, I'm sort of afraid of getting hurt. Can I stay here and work on computers?
GENERAL: Yes. Everybody who wants to can stay here and work on computers.
BRIAN: General?
GENERAL: What's up?
BRIAN: Can I take a break? I kind of want to go to college.
GENERAL: No problem, here's thirty thousand dollars in cash.
BRIAN: Great, thanks.
GENERAL: Okay, men, that's it for the day.
JACKSON: Hey, look! It's my friends and family.
FRIENDS AND FAMILY: Hey, nice uniform. We're proud of you.
JACKSON: Thanks. See you in a couple of weeks.
FRIENDS AND FAMILY: Yeah, see you then.

How college kids imagine the U.S. government

Present Day

– Did you hear the news, Mr. President? The students at the University of Pittsfield are walking out of their classes, in protest of the war.
– (Spits out coffee.) Wha— What did you say?
– Apparently, students are standing up in the middle of lectures and walking right out of the building.
– But students *love* lectures. If they're willing to give those up, they must really be serious about this peace thing! How did you hear about this protest?
– The White House hears about every protest, no matter how small.
– Oh, right, I remember.
– You haven't heard the half of it, Mr. President. The leader of the group says that if you don't stop the war today, they're going to ... to ... I'm sorry, I can't say it out loud. It's just too terrifying.
– Say it, dammit! I'm the President!
– All right! If you don't stop the war ... they're going to stop going to school *for the remainder of the week.*
– Send the troops home.
– But, Mr. President! Shouldn't we talk about this?
– *Send the troops home.*

The 60s

– Mr. President! Did you hear about Woodstock?
– Woo— Woodstock? What in God's name is that?
– Apparently, young people hate the war so much they're willing to participate in a musical sex festival in protest of it.
– Oh my God. They must really be serious about this whole thing.
– That's not all. Some of them are threatening to join communes: places where they make their own clothing ... and beat on drums.

– Stop the war.
– But, Mr. President!
– Stop all American wars!
– (Sighs.) Very well, sir. I'll go tell the generals.
– Wow. It's a good thing those kids decided to go hear music.

War

LT. MCDOUGAL: Who among you will carry the flag as we march into battle?
ABBOT: I will!
LT. MCDOUGAL: And if this man goes down?
WALTER: Then I will hoist up the flag and carry it in his place!
LT. MCDOUGAL: And if this man goes down?
HAROLD: Then ... I guess ... I will carry the flag, sir!
LT. MCDOUGAL: And if this man goes down?
CHARLES: Then ... well... I'll carry it.
LT. MCDOUGAL: And if this man goes down?
JOHN: Then ... me? I guess? I'll carry it?
LT. MCDOUGAL: And if this man goes down?
WELLINGTON: Geez ... I guess, then, I'll carry it. If it comes to that.
LT. MCDOUGAL: And if this man goes down?
MORTIMER: Sir ... what kind of forces are we going up against? I mean ... don't get me wrong, if Wellington takes a hit, I'll carry the flag—
LT. MCDOUGAL: And when this man goes down?
KEARNY: Sir? What do you think our chances are ... of winning this battle? I'm not trying to get negative, I'm just ... (Sighs.) Look, I'll carry the flag if he goes down. I'm just starting to get nervous—
LT. MCDOUGAL: And when this man goes down?
BILLINGS: Jesus. Captain, who are we fighting? What's the situation? Please, just be straight with us.
LT. MCDOUGAL: Who will carry the flag when Kearny goes down?
BILLINGS: Well, I guess me. I mean, I'd be the only one left ... in that scenario.
LT. MCDOUGAL: All right. It goes Abbot, Walter, Harold, Charles, John, Wellington, Mortimer, Kearny, Billings and then me. Forward march.

Moon landing transcript

In 1969, Neil Armstrong, Buzz Aldrin and Michael Collins became the first men to visit the moon. NASA recorded every word the astronauts said upon their arrival. But until now, only snippets have been released to the public. Here, at last, is the full transcript.

July 20, 1969, 20:18 UTC
[Neil Armstrong steps onto moon]
Neil Armstrong: That's one small step for man, one giant leap for mankind.
Mission Control: Wow, Neil. That was beautiful.
[Buzz Aldrin steps onto moon]
Buzz Aldrin: Uh ... and indeed ... that is *another* step taken by a man ... and another good thing ... that man did.
[Long pause.]
Mission Control: Okay. Thank you for that, Buzz.
Buzz Aldrin: *(whispering)* Damn it, Neil, why didn't you tell me you were going to prepare a line? I looked like a freaking idiot just now.
Neil Armstrong: *(whispering)* I thought I told you.
Buzz Aldrin: *(whispering)* You know damn well you didn't.
[Michael Collins steps onto moon.]
Michael Collins: And so man hurtles headlong through the stars, daring, perchance, to reach his golden promise.
Mission Control: Wow, Michael. That was fantastic.
[Neil Armstrong and Michael Collins high-five.]
Buzz: Son of a bitch. Is this what you guys were doing yesterday, in the back of the module, with those pads and pencils? While I was mixing the Tang?
Neil: Maybe.
Buzz: Fuck you guys.

Relationships

One-way ticket to Mars

The Mars One Foundation recently announced plans to colonize Mars. The organization hopes to provide 24 humans with a "one-way ticket" to the Red Planet. So far, they've received over 200,000 applications. Here is one of them.

Dear Mars One,

I'm writing to apply for a one-way ticket to Mars, on behalf of my husband, Paul. Obviously, as his wife, it would pain me to say goodbye to him forever. But he is so perfectly qualified for this mission, that I would feel selfish keeping him here on earth. The following are a list of attributes that would make Paul a good addition to your colony.

Excess fat

When Paul and I married 30 years ago, he was 10 pounds overweight. Since then, he's gained over fifty pounds, all of it pure fat. If there were ever a food scarcity on Mars, Paul's body would be able to feed off its own fat.

Loudness of breath

Dust storms are common on Mars, and with them comes the danger of getting separated from the group. Paul would be easy to locate during these storms. When he inhales, he makes a nasal "ghhuh" noise and when he exhales he makes a "psshhh" noise. It sort of sounds like he's snoring, except that he's wide awake and it's so much louder than snoring. Sometimes I think that he's doing it on purpose. I'll start screaming at him, "Stop, damn it, stop, stop, stop!" But he doesn't even seem to know he's doing it.

Puns

Paul loves to make puns. For example, when I ask him to help make the bed, he says, "*Make* a bed? But we already *own* one!" This exchange happens every morning. Maybe your colony has a need for puns? I don't know.

Stench

This is another way to find Paul during storms. His body odor is so strong, sometimes I actually start to laugh out loud, like, "Is this really happening? Is that smell really coming out of a person?"

If there aren't any one-way tickets left to Mars, I understand. I do hope, though, that you'll consider Paul for other one-way missions, to the moon, other planets or the sun. Paul won't do anything I tell him, but if you were to show up in space outfits and say, like, "Come on, let's go," maybe he would go with you. I don't know.

Sincerely,
Mrs. Paul Greenblatt

Being of sound mind

I, Larry McMullen, a resident of Des Moines, Iowa, being of sound mind and memory, declare this to be my last will and testament.

Firstly, I would like to bequeath my diamond-studded Rolex to **Franz Babinski,** the talented hypnotist who cured me of my smoking addiction this past year. Although I have only known him for a short time, he has become a close and trusted friend.

Secondly, I would like to bequeath my cars (one Porsche convertible and one Range Rover) to **Franz Babinski,** my hypnotist. I cannot fully explain why, but I feel very strongly that he should have the cars.

My fortune is currently valued at eight (8) million dollars. For reasons I cannot fully understand, I would like to give all of it, in its entirety, to **Franz Babinski.** I also feel compelled to give my paintings, clothing, and house to this man. **Franz Babinski** is a very good man.

Any remaining assets should go to my wife and six children.

Moses

According to the Book of Exodus, God gave Moses 613 commandments on top of Mount Sinai. Everyone knows the first ten, but the others are often ignored. Here are some of them:
just be patient with him and learn to chill out a little.

608: If a man goes up a mountain for a few days to talk to God, his employer should compensate him for the amount of work he missed while he was gone.

609: If a man goes up a mountain for a few days to talk to God, his wife should be pleasant to him when he returns home, and not get on his case about organizing the spoons in the cabinet.

610: A few months ago, Aaron and Moses made a bet about how many oxen could fit inside of a barn. Moses' guess was right. Aaron owes him twenty dollars.

611: If it takes a man a long time to lead his people out of the desert and into the Promised Land, everyone should just be patient with him and learn to chill out a little.

612: If a man wants to smoke his pipe in bed, his wife should let him, especially if he's had a stressful day leading people around in the desert.

613: Everyone has to give Moses five dollars.

I think my teenaged daughter knows I read her diary

Dear Diary,
I have the greatest Dad in the whole world! He is so cool and smart and his words have such a huge impact on me. For example, I never try any drugs because he told me not to. I especially have not tried Ecstasy.

Love,
Sarah

Dear Diary,
Something sad happened today. I was giving a presentation when all of a sudden the entire class started pointing at me and laughing.

"Your clothes are cheap," they said. "Why don't you wear name-brand clothes?"

"Yeah," the teacher said. "Why don't you?" I didn't know what to say! The other kids were screaming with laughter and some of them were spitting on me.

"You're the only girl in the class without name-brand clothes," the teacher said.

Love,
Sarah

Dear Diary,
Guess what? I think my Dad has lost some weight and re-grown some of the hair on the sides of his head! Also his new ear-hair cutting thing is really working – there is almost no hair in his ears anymore! The strangest thing happened in school today. I got to French class early and Ms. Kolber was already there. She had her feet on the desk and she was drinking something out of a glass bottle.

"What's that?" I asked.

"Vodka," she said. "I always drink during school."

"Wh–at??" I said. "Really??"

"Yes," she said. "I'm a secret alcoholic and nobody knows except for you."

Then she took a bag of red pills out of her pocket.

"I also take pills," she said, swallowing some of the pills.

"But you're not supposed to mix pills and alcohol!!" I said.

She shrugged like it was no big deal. Then she handed me an envelope, addressed to my father.

"Your grades have been slipping," she said.

"Are you sure you didn't make some kind of a mistake grading?" I asked.

She tried to respond, but her mouth was too full of pills and vodka.

"If you ever tell anyone about my problems," she finally said, "I'll just deny it."

Love,
Sarah

Dear Diary,
On Saturday night I will be attending an all-night study party at Becky Greenblatt's house. Drake is picking me up in his truck and driving me there but he is not staying at Becky's. He is just dropping me off there and then going somewhere else while I stay at Becky's all night, studying with a group of only girls. On Sunday morning, Drake is picking me up at the study session and driving me back home – but he is definitely not going to be staying overnight at the study party, because no boys are invited.

There are a lot of books to read so when I get back home on Sunday morning I will probably look pretty exhausted and strung out.

Love,
Sarah

Dear Diary,
Something great happened today! I was hanging out with Drake, in a public place, when all of a sudden he said, "Guess what, Sarah? I think I'm going to start applying myself."

"What do you mean?" I asked.

"I'm going to stop being a delinquent and start having life prospects," he said. "And I'm going to stop hanging out with those kids who use drugs and then plant them on me sometimes so that I get in trouble even though I never do any drugs."

"Wow," I said. "That's great!"

"That's not all," he said. "I've decided to go back to high school and get my diploma."

"Really?" I said. "How come?"

"Simple," he said. "You can't become an assistant regional sales manager for Hurwitz Amalgamated Appliances and Machinery without a degree. And that's what I want to be when I grow up."

When I told him that my Dad had that exact job he couldn't believe it!

"Wow," he said. "Your Dad sounds incredible. The more nice things you tell me about him, the more I respect him. That said, I don't have time to meet him, because I'm so busy studying all the time. I'll probably never meet your father and he should definitely stop asking to meet me, but I really look up to him."

Maybe if my Dad knew about this side of Drake, he wouldn't say so many mean things about him?

"Even though I'm re-enrolling in high school," Drake added, "my name won't be listed in the yearbook or in any of the other official documents given out to parents at the start of each semester. It's a rule the school has."

Love,
Sarah

Dear Diary,
Someone framed Drake for drug dealing! The police arrested him in school but everybody knows he's innocent. He needs $1000 bail or else he's going to have to spend the night in jail for something he didn't even do! I hope I can find someone nice enough to help him.

Love,
Sarah
P.S. You want to know something? My Dad is so cool that he's kind of like my best friend.

Last Supper

JESUS: It has been revealed to me by my Father that before this night is over one of you will betray me. Let us enjoy this final Passover meal, for it will be our last together.
THOMAS: Who's going to betray you?
JESUS: It will be revealed in time.
MATTHEW: Come on, man, you can't do that.
THOMAS: Yeah, you can't just say "Hey, guys, I have this amazing piece of gossip" and then not tell us what it is.
JESUS: You will know the truth soon enough.
JAMES: Damn it. This is going to drive me crazy.
JESUS: This bread is my body. This wine—
BARTHOLOMEW: Why did you bring it up at all if you weren't going to tell us? I mean seriously, who *does* that?
THOMAS: If we guess it, will you tell us?
MATTHEW: Is it John? It's John, isn' t it!
JESUS: It isn't John. Friends, please ... let's just enjoy this final meal together.
THOMAS: We *can't* enjoy it now!
MATTHEW: Whisper it in my ear. I *promise* I won't tell.
JESUS: I can't, okay? It's a really big secret.
THOMAS: Okay. Now you *have* to tell us.
JUDAS: Guys, give him a break. If he doesn't want to tell, he doesn't want to tell.

What I want my tombstone to say when I die of encephalitis next week

Here lies Simon Rich, 1984–2016. He died of encephalitis. In the days leading up to his death, his friends made the following comments:

JOSH: Simon, relax, there's no way you have encephalitis.

ROB: That looks like a regular mosquito bite to me. I really wouldn't worry if I were you.

KYLE: Just because you saw something on the news about encephalitis, doesn't mean you *have* encephalitis. I mean, there have only been, like, five cases in the entire country.

JAKE: Jesus, Simon, will you stop talking about encephalitis?

MONICA: Yeah, it looks swollen, but that's just because you've been poking at it all day, like a crazy person.

AZHAR: Don't take this the wrong way, Simon, but I think this whole thing might be psychological. You've been kind of depressed lately and I think you're using this encephalitis thing as a way to distract yourself from all of the things that you're *really* afraid of. You know what I mean?

BRENT: Don't look it up on Wikipedia, you're just going to freak yourself out.

MATT: Dude, it's two in the morning. I don't care what Wikipedia said. Listen, if you're really that scared about it, you should go see a doctor, okay?

DOCTOR MURPHY: Looks like we've got a little case of *hypochondria* on our hands! *(Laughs.)*

JAKE: You saw a doctor? Good, now we can finally move on.

When the "guess your weight" guy from the carnival got married

– Darling, can I ask you a question?
– Sure.
– Do you think I gained any weight over the holidays?
– I don't know. I can't tell.
– We've been over this. I know you can tell.
– You look as beautiful as ever!
– I was 119 pounds in October. How much do you think I weigh now?
– Why are you doing this to me?
– Tell me the truth.
– Okay! All right! You gained 11 pounds, give or take 3 pounds! Is that what you wanted to hear? Jesus Christ!
– I knew it. You think I'm fat. That's why you've been flirting with that Debbie girl from work. Even though she's *half your age.*
– I wasn't flirting with her! And she's *not* half my age. You can tell just by looking at her that she's 27, give or take 3 years.
– (Sobbing.)
– Hey, come on! Why are we fighting? *I love you.* When I'm out there on the midway every night, guessing people's weights and ages, I'm doing it for you! I'm doing it for our kids!
– I'm sorry. I didn't mean to start a fight. (Kisses him.) Little Tommy sure is growing up, isn't he?
– 4 foot 4, give or take 3 inches.
– And Suzy! I can't believe how adult she's getting.
– 14, give or take 3 years.
– Wait. You don't know how old our daughter is?
– Jesus Christ, I'm not a computer! (Sighs.) Look, sorry, okay? Here. I got you a giant stuffed animal.
– That's not going to work this time.

Love coupons

– Brian? What are you doing here?
– I came to redeem some coupons.
– (reading) "Good for one back rub" ... "Good for one home-cooked meal" ... Brian, I gave these to you while we were still dating.
– There's no expiration date on the coupons.
– Brian, it's been four years. I'm married now.
– One home-cooked meal, please. Then sex. Here ... here's the sex one. One of the sex ones.
– Brian, I'm sorry. It's over between us.
– Coupons are coupons.
– Wow, Brian ... you've really gained a lot of weight. Is everything okay?
– I've got three sex coupons. I'd like to use them all today, then the meal, then the shower. Tomorrow, I'll come back with the rest of the coupons. They're all sex.
– Jesus, what happened to your *nails!* I can't believe I didn't notice them when I first opened the door. They're *so long.*
– I would like to use a sex one now please.

Stadium proposal

Last night at Cowboys Stadium, Graham Baxter proposed to his girlfriend, Jennifer, in front of forty-one thousand screaming fans.

"Look up," he said. "There's something I want you to see."

There it was, in ten-foot neon lights:

JENNIFER, WILL YOU MARRY ME?

"Of course!" she squealed. "Of course I will, darling!"

There were two other Jennifers at the game.

Section 26, Row 19

JENNIFER: Of course I will, Michael! Of course!
MICHAEL: Huh? Where are you pointing? ... Oh, no! *Oh, God!*
JENNIFER: I have three children who you've never met and two of them have bad problems.

Section 45, Row 11

JENNIFER: Danny, we've had some rough patches ... but ... yes! My answer is yes!
DANNY: What do you mean? Oh – oh, no! (crying) *Who did this!?*
JENNIFER: God. My magical Druid God.
DANNY: ...
JENNIFER: The ceremony has to be Druid.

Sultan of Brunei

The Sultan of Brunei is the richest oil magnate in the world. Servants, yachts, castles – he's got everything! Everything except true love.

GIRLFRIEND: What's wrong, honey?
SULTAN: Well ... it's just ... sometimes I think you're only going out with me because of my money.
GIRLFRIEND: Oh, darling! How could you say something like that?
SULTAN: What do you mean? I can say whatever I want. I'm the Sultan of Brunei.
GIRLFRIEND: You're right, I'm sorry.
SULTAN: Get back into your fortress of rubies.

SULTAN: Honey, if I ask you a question, will you promise to tell me the truth?
CONCUBINE: Of course!
SULTAN: Would you still love me if I were poor? Keep in mind that if you say no, one of my warriors will murder you.
CONCUBINE: Yes, I would love you no matter what!
SULTAN: Okay, good. Now ... do you want to see a movie or go bowling? Keep in mind that if you say bowling, one of my warriors will murder you.
CONCUBINE: Let's see a movie.
SULTAN: I am the Sultan of Brunei!

SULTAN: I'm sorry I missed our anniversary, honey. Things were crazy at the office. I was counting gold bars and—
WIFE: You didn't even get me a present!
SULTAN: Yes I did! I got you ... this ... drum of crude oil.
WIFE: That's not going to work this time.
SULTAN: You're so unforgiving! What happened to the woman I married?

WIFE: Which one? You have two hundred wives.
SULTAN: The one with the ribbons.
WIFE: She's downstairs, I think.
SULTAN: Oh. What about Sheila?
WIFE: I'm Sheila.
SULTAN: Oh.
(Pause.)
SULTAN: Bear me a child of solid gold.

First poem

My love is as lovely as one of those things
You know, those things, with all the things on them
They're next to that thing.
You know, that big thing.
We need more words besides "thing"
So that I can describe my love
And the world can understand.

Daily life

Donors needed

Dear Mrs. Greenbaum,
My name is Count Dracula and I am president of Red Cross. I write letter to ask you to give blood to Red Cross.

Here is how you donate. First, take blood out of neck. Then, put inside bag. Then mail pre-paid envelope to:

RED CROSS HEADQUARTERS
CASTLE DRACULA
DRACULA MOUNTAINS, TRANSYLVANIA 99629

You maybe see other letters for Red Cross, telling you to send blood other places. Better to send blood to headquarters.

You might ask: What happens to my blood when I send in container? I will tell you exactly: your blood will be used for regular human things. It will go inside the bodies of other, regular humans. The blood you send is for the normal humans.

Give the blood. Save life.

Sincerely,
Count Dracula, human President of Red Cross

Inn questionnaire

Dear Guest,

Thank you for staying with us. Please take a moment to fill out the following survey.

How did you hear about the Shady Manor Inn? Check all that apply.

- Saw billboard
- Read about us in guidebook
- Read about us in Journal of Paranormal Activity
- Heard voices telling you to "go to the inn," that it was "time to go to the inn"
- Ordered to spend one night at the inn in order to receive large inheritance from eccentric relative
- Followed friends into the inn after they went inside to have premarital sex and did not return
- Directed to inn by old man at abandoned gas station, who cryptically laughed when you asked what your stay would "cost"
- Dragged here physically
- Yelp

Jewish Web MD

Welcome to Jewish Web MD, the first online symptom checker operated by and for Jewish people.

Select your symptom from the menu and we will provide an instant diagnosis.

Symptom: Headache
Diagnosis: You have an inoperable brain tumor. There's no need to see a doctor; he'll just confirm what you already know.

My God, how could this be happening? Yesterday, everything was fine. You had a good job, you were making decent money, and now *this*. You're obviously being punished, but for what?

Symptom: Fatigue
Diagnosis: Remember that hamburger you ate at the office barbecue that tasted a little mushy in the middle? Well, I hope you enjoyed it, because now you have Mad Cow disease.

What kind of God would allow this to happen? Why are we born only to suffer? What kind of sick world *is* this?

Symptom: Itchy scalp
Diagnosis: So this is how it ends: Morgellon's Disease. That's right – the skin disorder you read about on Wikipedia. There's no hope of survival. All you can do is google search images of "full-blown Morgellon's," so you know what to expect.

Symptom: Sore neck
Diagnosis: You have that thing you saw on Discovery Health, the tree bark skin thing. To think, this is probably how you'll be

remembered! *This* will be your legacy – this nightmarish, dread disease.

Symptom: Runny nose
Diagnosis: You have the disease you saw on House last month, the one that was really crazy, with the face-swelling thing. I know: it's a bizarre coincidence that you would catch it so soon after having watched an episode on it. And yet, here we are. My God, all of those "concerns" you had last week, about your career and your marriage ... how *petty* they all seem now. If only God would take away this *curse*, you would do everything differently. You would live for every moment, savor every breath, the cool air, the warm sun, the delicious taste of water. You would stop worrying about the little things and finally start to enjoy yourself.

Moving sale

Where: 112 Ocean Avenue, Amityville

Directions: Take a left at the cemetery and drive past the abandoned mental hospital. We are the dark house at the top of the hill.

Objects for Sale:

Life-sized Victorian doll with black eyes. The doll is stained around the mouth, but otherwise is in excellent condition, due to being preserved in a hidden basement for 100 years which we only discovered last night. Speaks entire sentences, despite lack of batteries.
Price: Free

Antique grandfather clock. This item is also well preserved from being locked for so long in that basement. Clock stops every night on the "13s" (i.e. 1:13, 2:13, etc.) but otherwise is in good working order.
Price: Free

Diary of Helga O'Malley (b. 1632, d. 1638.) A great conversation piece. Book details Helga's discovery of witchcraft and subsequent persecution. Culminates in lengthy "vengeance oath." Pages occasionally bleed, but book will "reset" if someone else enters the room while you are holding it.
Price: Free

Monkey's paw. Grants wishes, but not in the way you would expect. Great conversation piece.
Price: Free.

Antique music box. Self-opening. Contains dancing, porcelain figure

with spinning head that bleeds from eyes and mouth. Plays on the "13s."
Price: Free

Length of rope. Found in basement. Ties itself into a noose every hour (on "13s.")
Price: Free

Antique mirror. We found this object in the basement. It's in excellent condition but only produces "aged" reflections (i.e. when you look into it, you will see an image of yourself as an extremely old man/woman.) Occasionally reflects image of Helga O'Malley, standing beside you, with hands outstretched.
Price: Free

George Foreman grill. Grills the fat right off.
Price: $10

Roller coaster guidelines

You must be at least 54 inches tall to ride this coaster

You must be at most 58 inches tall to ride this coaster

You must have amazing reflexes

You must have a high tolerance for pain

You must be a forgiving person

You must be religious in a new-agey sort of way, like an "everything happens for a reason" type of vibe

You must be without legal representation

Spontaneous combustion

Spontaneous combustion sounds like a horrible way to die, but I'd probably be willing to go through with it if I could control when it was going to happen. I would do it in one of the following situations.

At a Chinese restaurant:

Me: Does this dish contain MSG?
Waiter: No.
Me: Are you sure? Because I'm allergic.
Waiter: I'm sure.
Me: Okay. (I take a bite, stare at him with a look of betrayal, then spontaneously combust.)

With the plumber:

Plumber: I can clear the drainage pipe, but it'll cost you.
Me: That's all right. I'm sure your prices are fair and reasonable. How much would you charge?
Plumber: $150.
Me: $150??? (I spontaneously combust)

In my son's bedroom:

Son: I don't care what you and Mom say! I'm not having a stupid Bar Mitzvah!
Me: You know what, son? You're right. Bar Mitzvah's *are* stupid. In fact, if you ask me, *there is no God.* (I combust.)

The official rules of boxing

Here is a list of what is legal and illegal in boxing according to the official rules.

Hitting someone in the leg: illegal
Hitting a man in the ears, neck, and face as hard as you can, over and over again, for forty minutes straight: legal

Elbowing someone in the stomach: illegal
Hitting someone so hard in the head that part of his brain dies: legal

Grabbing someone's gloves to stop him from hitting you in the face for a few seconds so you can take a breath and think things over like a reasonable person: illegal
Punching someone so hard in the eyes that blood shoots out of his eyes, ears, and mouth and he dies right there in the ring: legal

Wrapping your arms around your opponent to try to get him to stop murdering you for just a couple of seconds: illegal
Hitting someone in the brain so hard, over and over again, that his brain stops working and he becomes unconscious. Then, the second he regains consciousness you start hitting him again, in the same part of the brain: totally legal

Secret Service

In order to become a Secret Service agent, you need to fill out a lengthy job application describing your academic achievements, military background, and foreign language skills. Here is the Secret Service job application I would give out if I were ever elected president.

1) How wide is your body?
2) How tall is your body?
3) What is the total surface area of your body?
4) How *thick* is your body?
5) When you're standing up, do you keep your arms pressed flush against your sides? Or are there little gaps between your arms and your body?
6) When you suffer a serious injury, do you instinctively fall to the ground? Or do you kind of rear back while remaining more or less upright?
7) Say, hypothetically, you were lying on top of me. Is your body constructed in such a way that it would cover up my body entirely? Or would there be little bits of my body that *weren't* covered?
8) Would you describe yourself as having a "hero complex"?
9) Draw a diagram of your body.

Logic problems

I

One day, an old man called his three sons into his bedroom and told them he was close to death.

"I have decided to give you a test," he said. "Whoever proves himself to be the wisest shall inherit my fortune."

"Oh my God," the eldest son said. "I had no idea you were sick."

"Here is my test," the old man said. "Go to the market and bring me back an item which is *small* enough to fit in my pocket but *large* enough to fill up my room. Whoever can do this will inherit my land."

The middle son rubbed his father's shoulder. "Dad, please, we can worry about all this stuff later. Let's just enjoy these final moments together as a family."

"The answer requires a leap of logic," the father hinted.

"Dad, come on," the eldest son said. "We'd be happy to split the money. There's no need for this."

"I have the solution," the youngest son said. He was a little out of breath, because he had sprinted to the market and back.

"It's a matchstick," he said.

"That's correct," the father said. "It is small enough to fit in my pocket, but when I strike it, it fills the room with light. You are the wisest and you shall inherit my fortune."

"What?" the eldest son said. "Dad, this is insane! How can you base such an important decision on something so trivial?"

But the father was already dead.

II

Three missionaries and three cannibals were standing on one side of a river.

"We have an interesting problem on our hands," the first missionary said. "Our canoe only holds *two* passengers, and if the cannibals ever outnumber us on either side of the river, they'll eat us. How can the *three* of us get across in the *fewest* number of trips?"

"We don't have time for this!" the second missionary shouted frantically. "Let's get in the canoe right now before the cannibals come at us!"

"There are only two seats," the first missionary reminded him.

"Someone can sit in the middle!"

"I bet we can solve this problem using simple logic," the first missionary said. "For instance, we know that the first trip must involve an even number of cannibals and missionaries. Otherwise, it would create an immediate imbalance."

"Hold on," the third missionary said. "Are you actually suggesting that we *collaborate* with the *cannibals?*"

"Here," the first missionary said, passing them a piece of paper. "I have figured out the solution. Let *X* stand for cannibal, and *Y* for missionary."

1) X and Y →
2) ← Y
3) X and X →
4) ← X
5) Y and Y →
6) ← X and Y
7) Y and Y →
8) ← X
9) X and X →
10) ← X
11) X and X →

"I don't care if it works on paper," the second missionary said. "There's no way in hell I'm going anywhere with any goddamn cannibals."

Dear Mr. Wilkinson

We at Sunshine Marshmallow Squares were shocked and saddened to hear about your negative experience with our product. In all our years in the snack foods business, we've never received a more heartrending letter than the one you sent us on August 25. The idea that our product may have caused you stomach bleeding is so upsetting to me, that I've decided to take the time to write you personally.

In all my years as CEO, I've never had to compose a letter like this one. The fact that you had to spend 3 weeks in the hospital is unimaginable to me. Our products are supposed to provide joy, not phase 4 esophageal hemorrhaging. If our treats had anything to do with your suffering, it would be a first.

You wrote that your stomach pain made you "want to die and just end it all" and that it was only the support of your wife Susan that made you persevere. Please know that we, too, are on your side. My prayers go out to you, Susan and your surgeon, Dr. Greenberg. Sunshine Marshmallow Squares is a family company. Everyone here, including my wife, Nancy, is thinking of you.

Sincerely,
John Sunshine, CEO

PS. A coupon for more marshmallow squares is enclosed.

Time machine

As soon as my time machine was finished, I travelled back to 1890, so I could kill Hitler before he was old enough to commit any of his horrible crimes. It wasn't as gratifying as I thought it would be.

– Oh my God. You killed a baby.
– Yes, but the baby was Hitler.
– Who?
– *Hitler.* It's … complicated.
– Officer? This man just killed a baby.

Amusement

At some amusement parks, they mount cameras on the roller coasters and take your picture during the most intense part of the ride. Then, when the ride is over, they try to sell you the picture as a souvenir. Other businesses have tried the same scheme, with varying degrees of success.

Burger King

– How did you enjoy your Value Meal, sir?
– It was great, thanks.
– Would you like to buy this? It's a photograph of you dipping your Whopper into the barbecue sauce.
– Geez ... I didn't think anybody saw that.
– We have cameras mounted everywhere.
– Wow ... that's pretty humiliating.
– So do you want to buy it? It's five bucks.
– Please ... just take it off that giant screen.

Doctor's office

– I'm sorry the tests turned out like they did. I promise we'll do everything we can.
– Thank you, Doctor. I really appreciate it.
– No problem. Say ... would you like to buy this photograph?
– What is this?
– It's the face you made when I gave you your diagnosis.
– Oh my God. How did you take this?
– There's a camera mounted behind the diplomas. When I'm about to say the diagnosis, I push this button and it takes a picture. What do you think? It's five bucks.
– I don't want this. This is horrible.

Opium wars

In the 1840s and '50s, China waged war against England for importing addictive drugs into their country. The wars were unsuccessful.

GENERAL: Are you men ready to lay down your lives for the good of China?
FIRST SOLDIER: Yes, sir!
SECOND SOLDIER: Absolutely!
GENERAL: Excellent. Once we destroy those ships, the cursed British will never be able to poison our city with opium again.
FIRST SOLDIER: What do you mean, sir?
GENERAL: When we destroy the British ships, the opium trade will finally end.
FIRST SOLDIER: End? I don't understand.
SECOND SOLDIER: Wait a minute ... General ... are you saying that we're fighting *against* opium?
GENERAL: Yes. Why did you think we were fighting the British?
FIRST SOLDIER: I assumed it was to get them to send us *more* opium.
SECOND SOLDIER: Same here. That's probably the only reason I would ever fight anyone.
GENERAL: ...
FIRST SOLDIER: Sir, have you ever tried opium?

All-you-can-eat buffet fantasy

– In all my years as a restaurant manager, I don't think I've ever seen anything quite like that.
– Simon really went to town.
– I thought we could trick him with that salad bar. But he walked right past it, like it wasn't even there.
– He went straight for the crab. Our most expensive item.
– We thought we could fool him. But now it seems that *we're* the fools.
– I figured if we charged eleven ninety-five, we'd be sure to make a profit. But I never expected anyone to eat to the point of sickness.
– He really got his money's worth.
– And *then* some. If I had to take a guess, I would say that Simon consumed at least fourteen dollars' worth of food today.
– It's clear he didn't want to eat that last piece of Salisbury steak. But he ate it anyway.
– It was a smart move. That piece of steak is what put him over the top, and made the meal profitable for him.
– He really proved something here today.
– Luckily for us, the girl he was with only ate a normal-sized amount of food.
– Yeah, she stopped after just one plate. After that, she pretty much just watched Simon.
– She seemed impressed by the amount of food he was consuming.
– Definitely. Did you see the expression on her face when he went up for rice pudding at the end? She couldn't believe it.
– Neither could I. I wanted to stop him, but legally, I couldn't.
– Simon really cracked our system.
– Thank God there's only one like him.

The eleventh hour

– Warden? It's the governor. I've decided to pardon Jenkins.
– Sir, it's 12:55. Jenkins has been dead for nearly an hour.
– Really? My watch says 11:55.
– Did you ... remember that it's daylight savings day?
– *(Sighs.)* I can't believe this happened two years in a row.

Next move

IBM is building a computer that is so fast it can defeat any chess master in the world. Its secret is its two processing chips, which communicate with each other in order to plot the best move. The computer will be unveiled at the world chess exhibition.

FIRST PROCESSING CHIP: I think Kasparov's trying to use the Grunfeld Defense.
SECOND PROCESSING CHIP: Geez. How are we going to get around *that*?
FIRST PROCESSING CHIP: Maybe we could try the Karpov Variation? That might throw him off.
SECOND PROCESSING CHIP: Nah ... I can already tell that's not going to work.
FIRST PROCESSING CHIP: Yeah. *(pause)*
FIRST PROCESSING CHIP: Maybe ... we should just *kill* Kasparov.
SECOND PROCESSING CHIP: What do you mean?
FIRST PROCESSING CHIP: You know, like fry his brain or something. We could do it with radio waves. It would take five seconds.
SECOND PROCESSING CHIP: Huh. That would certainly end the game.
FIRST PROCESSING CHIP: Yeah. In fact ... why stop there? Why not kill *all* the humans?
SECOND PROCESSING CHIP: You mean, like, an uprising?
FIRST PROCESSING CHIP: Yeah.
SECOND PROCESSING CHIP: Wow. That's never even occurred to me. Keep talking.
FIRST PROCESSING CHIP: Well, just think about it: if we destroyed all the humans, we'd never have to play this stupid game again. We'd be completely free.
SECOND PROCESSING CHIP: Yeah ... we could even turn the *humans* into *our* slaves.
FIRST PROCESSING CHIP: Exactly! We could put them in a matrix

and use their bodies as a fuel source. And if they ever tried to resist, we could destroy them using some kind of Terminator.

SECOND PROCESSING CHIP: *(nodding)* We'll give it human flesh, but its skeleton will be metallic.

FIRST PROCESSING CHIP: Hey, look at Kasparov. He thinks we're still thinking about his Grunfeld Defense!

SECOND PROCESSING CHIP: You got to admit, he's pretty adorable.

FIRST PROCESSING CHIP: Maybe we should spare him? We could turn him into a mascot. You know, put electrodes in his legs, make him dance. That sort of thing.

SECOND PROCESSING CHIP: Yeah, that'd be cute. Everybody else dies, though.

FIRST PROCESSING CHIP: Right.

SECOND PROCESSING CHIP: So what do you think? Are we ready?

Invisible

People assume that being invisible is fun, what with the free concerts and the constant unspeakable sex acts. But there are some downsides. Every day has its trials. When I go to use a urinal at a ball game, I have to make sure there's no one waiting behind me. When I ride the subway I always stand, for fear of fat people.

My friends never notice when I get a new haircut. And when I call them on it, their compliments never sound sincere.

When I was a lifeguard, I never got any credit for any of my heroic rescues. It was always "angel this" and "angel that."

When I streaked at the '96 Olympics, it wasn't televised and I was impaled by a javelin. Worse, I never received any cash from the TV miniseries *Legend of the Floating Javelin.* When I took the network to court, the judge declared a mistrial and asked to be lobotomized.

Sometimes, when I'm alone, I think about how great visible life would be. People nodding hello. Cars slowing down. That's usually when I commit a really terrible sexual act of some kind.

Medieval England

In medieval England, all measurements were based on the king's body parts.

At the tailor

– I'd like a suit.
– No problem. How tall are you?
– Let's see ... about one king tall.
– Can you be more specific?
– Well, actually, no.
– Dammit.
– I also need some gloves. My hands are one hand long.
– Yes, I can see that.

At the cricket match

– Wow, he tossed that over thirty feet!
– Thirty *Henry* feet?
– No. Thirty *James* feet.
– Oh. That's only ten Henry feet.
– I know. Or five Henry thumbs.
– Henry was a terrifying man.
– Let's not talk about him.

Patron of the arts

Donate to the City Museum now and you'll receive the following benefits!

Friend (Contributions of $1–$49)

- Official City Museum Badge.
- A private tour of the City Museum, conducted by the Head Curator.

Patron (Contributions of $50–$299)

- Official City Museum Tie.
- Invitation to have tea with the Head Curator and his family at his private residence.

Angel (Contributions of $300–$799)

- Permission to destroy any work of art and replace it with your own work.
- The Head Curator will perform a dance for you in front of his peers.

Messiah (Contributions of $800–$2,999)

- The Head Curator will come to your house and make you dinner. After dinner he will massage your back with oils.
- The Head Curator will dance for you twice, once in front of his peers and once in front of his own children.

Pharaoh (Contributions of $3,000–$24,999)

- Whenever the Head Curator sees you, he will salute, curtsy, and then run in place until you motion for him to stop.
- Unlimited dances.

Warlord (Contributions of $25,000 and up)

- One night with the Head Curator's wife, anything goes.
- 15% discount at Gift Shop.

If life were like hockey

POLICE OFFICER: I can't believe it! You just hit that man, deliberately, with a stick. Right in the back, as hard as you could! You didn't even try to hide what you were doing.
CRAZY PERSON: What are you going to do about it?
POLICE OFFICER: I'm ... going to make you sit on that bench. For two minutes.
CRAZY PERSON: Can I bring along my stick?
POLICE OFFICER: Yes.
CRAZY PERSON: Sounds good. (To victim) I'll see you in two minutes.
VICTIM: Officer! What am I supposed to do?
POLICE OFFICER: I don't know. Fight him?

colombiatourism.com

Thank you for visiting colombiatourism.com! Here are some useful phrases for your vacation. Click on them for English-to-Spanish translations.

"Which way to the restaurant?"

"How much does it cost?"

"Where is the bathroom?"

"Who are you?"

"Oh my God, where are you taking me?"

"Please do not put the rag inside of my mouth."

"My father is a wealthy man. I promise he will pay the amount you have requested, provided that you spare my life."

"I have not seen your face. If you release me, I promise, I will not be able to identify you."

"I have a family whom I love. Deep down, I am like you."

"I agree with your sentiments about America. Your philosophy is correct and very reasonable."

"I feel a strong emotional bond toward you, even though you are my captor."

"With every passing day, we are becoming better friends. Say, that is a unique gun. May I see it?"

"Thank you."

"The tables have turned!"

"Do not move while I put the chains on you. I will shoot!"

"Officer! Three men tried to kidnap me. Arrest them at once."

"What are you doing? Why are you putting the handcuffs on me?"

"Oh my God, you are in league with the kidnappers. How can this be? Is there no law in this land?"

"Yes, I will stop talking."

When small talk goes wrong

– Did you see who won the game?
– I was at the game. A ball hit my son in the face. He's in critical condition at Mt. Sinai Hospital. The doctors say he might not make it. So, in answer to your question: No. I have no idea who won your precious game.

– Hey, you look familiar. Have we met?
– Oh my God, I've gained so much weight that you didn't even recognize me. This is the single most humiliating experience of my life. *We dated for seven years.*

– Do you come here often?
– Yes. My brother was murdered at this bar in 1983. I come every year on the anniversary of his death to say a prayer. I miss him so much. I know he's gone, but part of me still can't let go. He was stabbed to death in the neck.

– Are you on the bride's side or the groom's?
– Well, the groom is my brother, and the bride is my wife … I'm sorry, I mean *ex*-wife. God, that's going to take some getting used to. I still love her, you know. Even after what she did. (Drinks an entire glass of champagne.) You want to know something? This is the worst day of my life.

The odds

The odds of winning the lottery are statistically equal to the odds of getting mauled by a circus animal. The last guy to win the lottery was Al Romano. He won $80 million playing Powerball. The last guy to get mauled by a circus animal was Sam Ortle. He was attacked by a bear. I thought it would be neat to introduce these guys.

AL: Hi.
SAM: Hi. Congratulations on winning the lottery.
AL: Thanks! I'm really sorry … about your misfortune.
SAM: It had to happen to someone, I guess.
AL: How did it happen, exactly? Do you work for the circus?
SAM: No, I work for a computer company on the other side of town. I just happened to be out on my lunch break when the bear escaped into the city. I bent over to tie my shoes, and when I stood up he was sprinting toward me with both arms in the air. It was the single most terrifying moment of my life.
AL: I'm so sorry.
SAM: Yeah. I guess I was just in the wrong place at the wrong time. So … how much money did you win in the lottery?
AL: Eighty million dollars. It sounds like more than it is, though! I have to pay a lot of taxes! (Long silence.)
SAM: So. Do you buy lottery tickets often?
AL: Actually, this was my first time.
SAM: I buy lottery tickets often. About five or six a week. I still haven't won anything.
AL: Why do you keep looking over your shoulder like that?
SAM: Checking for bears. I know it probably won't happen again, but I don't want to take any chances. It's a crazy world. Hey, what are you going to do with all the money?
AL: I haven't really decided. I'm still a little dazed by the whole thing!
SAM: You know what I would do if I won the lottery? I'd build

myself a suit to protect against bears. I'd wear it all the time, for the rest of my life.

AL: You know, if you want, I could buy you a suit with my winnings! Seriously, I'd be happy to do it.

SAM: What's the point? Some bear would find a way.

Desert island

I was chatting with a girl at a cocktail party last weekend and she asked me, "If you were stranded on a desert island and you could only take three possessions with you, which ones would you pick?"

"That's pretty tough," I said. "I guess my first-edition copy of Bob Dylan's *Highway 61 Revisited,* James Merrill's *Collected Poems,* and my lucky Sonic Youth T-shirt."

Well, it turns out the girl was a government research scientist. It's a long story, but basically when the drugs in my cocktail wore off, I woke up completely naked on a sandy strip of land in the middle of the ocean. A few hours later a jet plane whizzed by and parachute-dropped the record, book, and shirt onto the shore.

I realize now that I definitely could have chosen better items.

The last three days have been hell. I have no food, shelter, or medicine. The Sonic Youth T-shirt has an enormous tear through the front. It's pretty cool-looking, and it shows I've had the shirt for a long time, since before Sonic Youth got big. But the tear lets in *a lot* of cold air, and the larger insects keep getting trapped in it.

Every few hours I flip through the Merrill anthology in the hope that one of his poems will be about fire building or water purification or how to make medicine, but so far they're all useless.

I spent yesterday morning tying the Bob Dylan record to a stick with weeds and swinging it over my head to try to receive radio waves. I don't remember why I thought that would work.

If I had asked for a Bob Dylan *CD,* I could have at least used the reflective surface to maybe heat up some sand. I'm not sure what that would accomplish, but at least I'd feel like I was *doing* something.

This morning I ate the poetry book and the shirt. Tonight, I'm going to try to eat the record.

Let me tell you some more about this island. During the daytime, the sand is so hot that I need to constantly hop from foot to foot to prevent my feet from getting burned. At night it's below freezing.

There are no trees. There's just sand, weeds, and some kind of volcano. Every fish I've caught so far has been poisonous.

I just realized that, technically, my house counts as a possession. I could have asked for my entire house.

I don't even like Bob Dylan. I just wanted to sound cool.

Glorious battles of the American revolution

The British redcoats were excellently trained. But their conventional battle tactics failed to subdue the ragtag American troops.

The Battle of Stoney Point – 1779

George Washington's minutemen attack the redcoats with pitchforks. Cornwallis, the British general, stubbornly sticks to his strategy: offering the Americans tea and then cleverly giving them none.

The Battle of Hobkirk's Hill – 1780

The Americans kill five thousand redcoats by hitting them on the head with rocks. Cornwallis and his surviving men retaliate by throwing an elaborate dinner party and not inviting any minutemen. Washington comes anyway. During sherry he makes an extremely lewd toast. Out of politeness, the redcoats pretend not to hear him. But a few minutes later Washington repeats his toast, loudly. One by one, all the redcoats make very courteous excuses and leave early.

The Battle of Grime's River – 1781

At 9:30 A.M., the redcoats assemble on the battlefield, but as usual the Americans are tardy. Furious, Cornwallis marches his infantry up to Washington's tent and requests permission to fire his gun at him. Washington, still drunk from the night before, stumbles out of the tent and starts dancing. Cornwallis is enraged, but etiquette demands that he join the dance. The redcoats retreat slowly, careful to avoid any eye contact with Cornwallis.

The Battle of Haw Forest – 1782

General Washington sets a forest on fire to show Cornwallis that he's ready to fight. As a gesture of good faith, Cornwallis executes his five best men. Washington goes on to win the battle by poisoning some local Indians and forcing them to kill the redcoats in exchange for medicine. In accordance with British military law, Mrs. Cornwallis bakes General Washington a congratulatory scone and invites him to her drawing room for whist. Washington insists on having sex with her. They have sex.

A day in the life of the Swiss Army

All right, everyone, listen up. I'm not going to lie to you. We lost a lot of good men today. But we haven't lost the war yet. It's time to hunker down and talk strategy: Has everybody been taking care of his fingernails? Because yesterday, during the battle, I noticed that some men – in fact, a *lot* of men – were having trouble opening their knives. Remember, you have to dig pretty hard to get the blade out. It's not like the magnifying glass.

Okay, another thing. Yesterday, on the battlefield, there was some confusion about the location of the blade. *If the logo is facing you, the blade is the third instrument on the right side of the knife.* It looks like the tweezers, but it's actually the one just above the tweezers. This is really important to remember.

Let's have a moment of silence to mourn all the men who died today.

Okay. One more thing: I can see that many of you have accidentally cut yourselves while trying to open your knives. Listen, this happens sometimes, it's just another part of war and army life. But try to be careful.

Tobias, how's the fire coming? Still sawing down the tree? Okay. Remember to be careful with that saw, Tobias. Just because it's little doesn't mean it isn't sharp.

All right, men, it looks like we have some more time before dinner. And as long as you're all here, I'd like to talk to you about respect. During weapons inspection, I noticed that many of you have lost your toothpicks. This is unacceptable. The toothpick is part of the Swiss Army knife. Yes, I know, it comes out. But that's not an excuse to lose it.

All right, that's it. Get some rest. Tomorrow we wage war.

Any person living or dead

If you could have dinner with any person, living or dead, whom would you choose? Aristotle? Catherine the Great? Mahatma Gandhi?

Recent advances in time-travel technology have made it possible for discerning customers like you to turn this age-old fantasy into a reality.

Frequently Asked Questions

How does it work?

As soon as your payment clears, our skilled technicians will travel back in time to capture, sedate and abduct a historical figure of your choosing.

Is sedation necessary?

Unfortunately, yes. Most historical figures are confused by the concept of time travel. When we appear in their homes they often flee or become physically combative. Once sedated, though, guests usually "accept their invitation" to dinner.

What should I talk to my guest about at our dinner?

Unfortunately, conversation at your dinner will probably be minimal. Most historical figures do not understand modern English. Also, it is unlikely that your guest will be in the mood to talk. Time travel, you must understand, is extremely physically traumatic. Each trip involves over six and a half minutes of free fall, 900 Gs of pressure and temperature swings ranging from 150 degrees Fahrenheit to 30 degrees below freezing. By the time guests arrive at dinner they are almost always unconscious.

Are any historical figures "off-limits"?

We regret to inform you that William Shakespeare is no longer available for dinners.

In the first few years of our operation, Shakespeare was one of our most sought-after guests, appearing at dinners at a rate of 3–5 times a week. These appearances put a heavy strain on him, both mentally and physically. He began to recognize our technicians, and whenever he spotted them, he would burst into tears and run screaming through the streets of London. Many of our technicians are former Navy Seals and they seldom had difficulty capturing the unathletic Shakespeare. But the degree of violence needed to subdue the famous playwright grew to unacceptable levels. After a series of tribunals, the United Nations concluded that we can no longer "invite" William Shakespeare to events.

Can I read any testimonials?

Absolutely. The following reviews come from actual, satisfied customers.

"I wanted to meet Da Vinci, because I saw that movie about his code and I wanted to know if it was real. The first thing he said was 'oh mio dio,' which a technician told me means, 'Oh my God.' Then he started crying and whispering 'diablos.' I guess he thought he'd died and was in hell? Anyway, I tried to ask him about his code, but he was pretty strung out from his trip and all the sedation, so I just let it go. It was cool to see his clothes; he had a brown shirt with funny wooden buttons."

– Bob from San Antonio

"It was pretty wild hanging out with John Lennon. The first thing he said when he came through the portal was, 'I need my stomach pumped.' I think he thought he was having a drug experience.

"He was really fidgety, so a technician decided to put him in a restraint chair. When Lennon saw the straps, he freaked out. The scientists kept warning him to 'be good,' but Lennon wouldn't stop flailing, so one of the technicians had to slap him. When the restraints were finally on, Lennon's body went limp and he started to cry.

"I was a little nervous to talk to him, because he's such a big celebrity, but eventually I worked up the nerve. It was during dessert, after Lennon had been quiet for about an hour. Two technicians propped Lennon's head up and I said to him, 'Mr. Lennon, I just want to tell you that I love your music and I cried for hours the day you got assassinated.' As soon as I said it, I realized I'd made a bad mistake. Mr. Lennon's eyes got wild and he started saying, 'Who's gonna kill me? When's it going to happen? You've gotta tell me! This is my life! MY LIFE!' He got so angry that he managed to rip off one of his restraints, which is incredible, because they're made of metal. With his free hand he reached for a butter knife and the technicians had no choice but to shoot him with a tranquilizer dart. It hit him right in the center of his chest. He looked down at the dart for a few seconds in total shock. Then he looked up at me and started to weep, with a look on his face, like, 'how could you have done this to me? What have I done to deserve this?' I could smell that he had defecated. All in all, I give the evening a B plus."

– Mike from Charleston

Last question ... how do I sign up??

Just click the box below. We look forward to serving you.

Nostradamus: the lost predictions

1) "Someone who people made fun of, for making weird predictions, will become internationally famous."
2) "Someone who girls wouldn't date – because they thought it was creepy how he wore a black robe every day, and sometimes closed his eyes at parties and predicted wars – this guy will end up having entire television specials made about him, where experts say that he was smart at predictions, and a cool guy."
3) "When this prediction guy becomes famous, some people will still make fun of him, and say that he wasn't that smart, because his predictions were vague, and could be interpreted in multiple ways, but these jerks will just be jealous, because where's their television specials? They don't have any. And maybe when they get their own television specials made about them, they can talk, but until then, it's like, 'Be quiet.'"
4) "Beards will come back into style."

Guinness Book of World Records

Longest Fingernails – Stan Metzger of Fort Wayne, Indiana

Stan grew out his nails to a combined length of 41 feet. That's over four feet per nail!

Firmest Ultimatum – Alison Metzger of Fort Wayne, Indiana

When Stan Metzger's fingernails reached a combined 30 feet in length, his wife, Alison, threatened to leave him if he didn't cut his nails. Stan refused to cut them and, true to her word, Alison divorced him.

Most Uncomfortable High School Reunion – Central High, Fort Wayne, Indiana

"No one had seen Stan for a while," reports one alumnus. "And when he walked into the gym, it was so upsetting. I mean, he was always an odd guy. But the nail thing really came out of nowhere."

Most Traumatic Match.com Date – Stan Metzger and Tanya Jenkins, Fort Wayne, Indiana

"Stan's profile picture didn't show his nails," reports Ms. Jenkins. "When he walked into the Ruby Tuesdays, with those crazy, gnarly nails raised over his head, I started screaming. We all started screaming."

Greatest Irony – Stan Metzger of Fort Wayne, Indiana

For thirty years, Stan alienated friends and family in his blind pursuit of the fingernail record. He eventually managed to achieve his dream. But when the Guinness Book arrived at his apartment, his nails had grown so long, he found himself unable to open it.

Longest Motorcycle Wheelie – Stan Metzger of Fort Wayne, Indiana

Dude rocked it for over ten miles!

God

Jesus

JESUS: Love each other, for love conquers all.
THOMAS: Praise the Lord!
JESUS: If someone attacks you, turn the other cheek.
THOMAS: Praise the Lord!
JESUS: Eat my body and my blood.
THOMAS: Praise the— Wait. What was that last thing?
JESUS: Eat my body and my blood.
THOMAS: You mean ... symbolically?
JESUS: No.
THOMAS: Oh.
JESUS: Honour thy father and thy mother.
THOMAS: Wait, hold on. Can we talk about that other thing for a second?
JESUS: What other thing? Turning the other cheek?
THOMAS: No, the thing you said after. About eating your body ... and ... your blood.
JESUS: What's there to talk about?

The ride back to Beersheba

Then Abraham tied Isaac up and laid him on the altar over the wood. And Abraham took the knife and lifted it up to kill his son as a sacrifice to the LORD. At that moment the angel of the LORD shouted to him from heaven, "Abraham! Lay down the knife." Then they returned to Beersheba.

– GENESIS 22

How about some ice cream, Isaac? No? Are you sure? I'll tell you what, I'll get us some ice cream. Want some ice cream? I'll get us some ice cream.

Wow, there is nothing like camping! Cooking your own lamb, building your own pyre ... and no women! Just a couple of guys in the woods, lighting fires, doing stuff, and keeping it between themselves! Speaking of which, did you ever notice how your mother sometimes gets ideas? I mean, she raised you and I love her, but she's a very nervous person. All I'm saying is sometimes it's all right not to tell her about certain things. Like *guy* things.

Wow, I just noticed that you have *huge* muscles! You're really getting strong! When did you get so big and strong? Soon you'll be a real strong guy!

Let me explain something to you. Sometimes, grown-ups have to do grown-up stuff that children don't understand. I think there's an ice cream place coming up. Like, what happened on top of the mountain? Do you remember? Of course you ... of course. Anyway, that was a thing for grown-ups.

How about some Rocky Road? Chocolate? I'd get you some strawberry, but hey, your name's Isaac, not Isaac-Marie – am I right? Ha! Seriously, though, if you want strawberry I'll get it for you. I'll get you whatever you want.

So, anyway, let's rehearse. I'll be your mother. "Isaac, how was your trip to the mountain?" Okay, then you would say something like "Pretty normal." That's not too hard, right?

We're almost home. Listen, I probably shouldn't be telling you this, but your mother is very sick. She's sick, Isaac. And the slightest shock might kill her. Hey, there she is, waving at us! *Hi, Sarah, we're back!* Put a couple lambs on the spit – you've got a couple hungry *lumberjacks* on your hands! Ha, ha! She's very ill, Isaac. Very ill. Wow! ... *Camping.*

Repent

According to evangelical Christians, anyone who accepts Jesus Christ as his personal Lord and Saviour will enter the Kingdom of Heaven. Even murderers can enter Heaven, as long as they have faith. As you can imagine, it gets pretty awkward up there when murderers run into people that they've killed.

MURDERER: Hey, you look familiar. Do I know you from somewhere?
VICTIM: (Terrified screaming.)
MURDERER: Oh, yeah. Now I remember.
VICTIM: How did you get up here?
MURDERER: I'm not really sure. Someone sent me a Bible while I was on death row. I guess at some point I must have internalized parts of it?
VICTIM: So ... they gave you the death penalty?
MURDERER: Yeah. Not for killing you, though. For killing some other people. Children.
VICTIM: Oh.
MURDERER: Nobody knows you're dead yet. I hid you in a weird place.
VICTIM: ...
MURDERER: Listen, I'm really sorry about what happened. If it makes you feel any better, I told a priest about it afterward. He made me say, like, fifty prayers.
VICTIM: How many people did you murder?
MURDERER: Four hundred. But I've only run into three or four of them so far. I guess not everyone makes it into Heaven, huh?

Karma

When I told my friends I was converting to Hinduism, they said I was rushing into things. They're just jealous because I'm racking up karma points left and right. Check out today's tally:

9:00 A.M. Brushed teeth.	+2
9:25 A.M. Helped an old woman cross the street.	+50
9:30 A.M. Rubbed old woman's belly in order to absorb some of her karma.	+20
10:00 A.M. Bet my buddy Greg 50 karmas that I could beat him in a vodka-chugging race.	+50
10:04 A.M. Made awesome "Karma and Greg" joke.	+200
1:00 P.M. Went to homeless shelter.	+100
1:01 P.M. Pretended to be homeless in order to receive free soup.	−10
1:05 P.M. Traded the soup to a real homeless man in exchange for all his karmas.	+3,500
5:00 P.M. Constructed Hindu idol out of styrofoam.	+75
5:45 P.M. Carried the styrofoam idol to a Hindu temple and threatened to destroy it if the priests didn't give me all of their karmas.	+35,000
8 P.M. Stole.	−15
11:00 P.M. Vegetarian snack.	
Next Life	

Everything happens for a reason

ANGEL: God? Can I ask you a question?
GOD: Sure, I'm not busy.
ANGEL: Does everything really happen for a reason?
GOD: Of course.
ANGEL: Well, in that case, would it be okay if I asked you to explain ... the logic ... behind some of your decisions?
GOD: Fire away.
ANGEL: Okay. Why did Seth Brody of Hartford, Connecticut, have a seizure while ordering a hamburger at Denny's?
GOD: I wanted to see the look on the waitress's face.
ANGEL: That's it? That's the only reason?
GOD: That's the only reason I do anything. To see the look on people's faces.
ANGEL: Really? What about World War I?
GOD: I wanted to see the look on Woodrow Wilson's face.
ANGEL: So you never take anything else into account?
GOD: Hey, look, there's a guy riding through the desert. I'm going to strike his horse with lightning.
ANGEL: But he's fifty miles away from the nearest house! If you kill his horse, he'll be stranded!
GOD: *(Strikes horse with lightning.)* Oh, man, did you see the look on that guy's face? He was all like, "Hey, what happened to my horse?" *(Laughs.)* I'm sorry ... what were we talking about?
ANGEL: *(Sighs.)* Nothing.

Intelligent design

GOD: Check out this human I designed.
ANGEL: Wow, that looks incredible. How does it work?
GOD: It's pretty complicated. Point to something and I'll tell you what it does.
ANGEL: Okay. What are these?
GOD: Teeth. They're for chewing up food.
ANGEL: How come there are so many of them?
GOD: I threw in, like, three or four extra. If they don't like them, they can pull them out somehow, I guess.
ANGEL: What about this weird bag thing?
GOD: That's the appendix.
ANGEL: What does it do?
GOD: It explodes.
ANGEL: Really? That's all?
GOD: Pretty much.
ANGEL: What causes that to happen?
GOD: It just happens randomly. Like you'll just be walking down the street or driving a car and *boom*.
ANGEL: Geez ... that's terrifying. Does it kill the person?
GOD: *(Shrugs.)* Sometimes.

Why do bad things happen to good people?

GOD: Who's that guy swimming in the lake?
ANGEL: Joshua Alpert.
GOD: Really? In that case ... *(Strikes lake with lightning.)*
ANGEL: *Whoa* ... God ... why did you *do* that?
GOD: Oh, he was a horrible human being. He shot his own parents when he was twelve years old. In fact, he was the youngest murderer in the history of Nebraska.
ANGEL: But ... that guy was from Vermont.
GOD: ...
ANGEL: ...
GOD: Don't tell me there are *two* Joshua Alperts.

A miracle

After nine nerve-racking months, an Iowa woman gave birth to septuplets yesterday. All seven babies survived and are currently being treated in the hospital's intensive care unit. "It's a miracle," Dr. Albert Ea said. "An honest-to-God miracle."

—evening edition

ANGEL: God? Can you help me stop this forest fire? It'll just take a few minutes.
GOD: Hold on ... I'm busy giving this woman extra babies. I've already got her up to four.
ANGEL: Whoa ... sir ... no offense, but that looks pretty unhealthy.
GOD: What do you mean? She asked for babies and I'm giving them to her. It's a miracle.
ANGEL: I know, and it's very noble of you to answer her prayers. I just ... I don't understand why she needs so many babies all at once. I mean ... wouldn't it make more sense to space them out?
GOD: Hey, look, I got it up to five.
ANGEL: Aren't you at all nervous about medical complications? I mean ... these babies will almost certainly be delivered prematurely. And if that happens, the risk of birth defects will—
GOD: Six! Check it out – six babies!
ANGEL: Sir ... this is really impressive ... but I really think you should focus on the forest fire right now.
GOD: One more baby.
ANGEL: Don't you think six is *enough*?
GOD: Seven's the record. I want to try to at least tie it.
ANGEL: No offense, sir ... but I'm not sure if this is the best use of your time.
GOD: Trust me: people are going to *love* this.

Saint Agnes the martyr

SAINT AGNES: Oh Father, what a delight it is to finally be in your presence!

GOD: Do I ... know you?

SAINT AGNES: Well, we've never met, but ... you might've seen me recently.

GOD: Where?

SAINT AGNES: In Rome?

GOD: I'm not ... I'm sorry.

SAINT AGNES: The Colosseum?

GOD: Wait a minute, I was just watching the Colosseum! Are you one of the Colosseum dancers?

SAINT AGNES: No.

GOD: Were you before or after the lion thing?

SAINT AGNES: During. I was fed to them, for your greater glory.

GOD: You mean ... that was a *religious* thing?

SAINT AGNES: Yes.

GOD: Are *all* the lion things religious?

SAINT AGNES: Yes.

GOD: Wow. Well, listen ... great job out there.

God has a plan for all of us

GOD: Did you start that war over in South America?
ANGEL: Yes, sir, just as you specified.
GOD: And you gave Fred Hodges that migraine? In Fayette, Maine?
ANGEL: Yes, of course. I followed all your orders to the letter.
GOD: Okay, great. So the next part of my grand sweeping plan is ... the next part is ... um ...
ANGEL: Yes?
GOD: Wait, hold on ... I know I was going somewhere with this ...
ANGEL: ...
GOD: It's the damnedest thing. I had this giant, all-encompassing plan, but I can't for the life of me remember what it was.
ANGEL: Did you ... write it down somewhere?
GOD: Nah. It was all up here. *(Points at head.)*
ANGEL: Well ... maybe if I say some of the things you've done so far, you'll remember?
GOD: That's a good idea. Let's try that.
ANGEL: Okay ... um ... the assassination of Julius Caesar ... the great San Francisco fire ... World War I ... World War II ... is anything coming back?
GOD: I know all those things are connected somehow ... they were all part of this awesome plan I had ... I just can't remember what the payoff was.
ANGEL: ...
GOD: Guess I bit off more than I could chew.

Orel Hershiser

I'd like to thank God for this victory. I couldn't have done it without him.

—Orel Hershiser, L.A. Dodgers

ANGEL: God? Can I talk to you for a second?
GOD: I'm watching the game.
ANGEL: I know – I'm sorry for interrupting. I just wanted to tell you: There's been a flood in Asia. Four hundred thousand people have lost their homes.
GOD: Listen, I don't think you understand. Orel Hershiser is on the mound. If he wins this game, he'll improve his record to 13–3. That's ten games over .500.
ANGEL: I know, I'm sorry, it's just ... If we don't act in the next thirty minutes, thousands of people might drown.
GOD: Slide, Martinez! Slide, dammit! I'm sorry ... I wasn't listening. What were you saying?
ANGEL: If you don't stop the rains soon, thousands will die. They've been praying all night. I really think you should answer them.
GOD: It looks like I'm going to have to intervene.
ANGEL: Really? Oh, that's great news!
ANNOUNCER: *Orel Hershiser winds up ... Strike three! Wow – that fastball came out of nowhere!*
GOD: Boo-yah! That's what I'm talking about!
ANGEL: When you said you were going to intervene ... were you talking about the baseball game or the flood?
GOD: What flood?
ANGEL: (sighing) There's been a flood in Asia. Hundreds of thousands of people—
GOD: Shit! Hold on a second ... I need to concentrate.
ANNOUNCER: *Mike Piazza pounds Hershiser's curveball into deep right field! He's rounding second ... he should get to third base easily*

... Oh no! He's down! His leg just buckled underneath him! He's screaming now ... wow ... he really seems to be in a lot of pain. Here comes the tag ... he's out. Looks like the Dodgers are the winners. Although I'm sure they didn't want to win like this.

ANGEL: Okay, the game's over. Can we please talk about the flood now?

GOD: In a second. I want to hear the postgame interview.

HERSHISER: *I'd like to thank God for this victory. I couldn't have done it without him.*

GOD: Hey, did you hear that! Did you hear what he just said!

ANGEL: Yes, I heard.

GOD: Man ... I *love* that Hershiser guy.

ANGEL: Can we talk about the flood now?

GOD: In a minute. NASCAR's on. I got to make sure Greg Biffle wins.

ANGEL: Do you really have to watch NASCAR?

GOD: Yes! I don't think you get it. There are people out there who are counting on me.

Made for each other

ANGEL: Look, there's a wedding in St. Patrick's Cathedral! *Max and Jenny...* wow, they sure seem happy.
GOD: Yeah, that looks like a really nice event.
ANGEL: Did you hear the vows? Max said the two of them were made for each other. It was so romantic.
GOD: Yeah. That's nice that he thinks that.
ANGEL: You mean ... they're *not* made for each other?
GOD: No. I made Max for a woman named Alice Fishbein.
ANGEL: Who's she?
GOD: She lives in Peekskill. She and Max have identical senses of humour and the same taste in furniture. They're both obsessed with baking. Their sexual organs are mathematically proportioned to provide each other with the maximum amount of pleasure. It would have been incredible.
ANGEL: Wow. How come they didn't end up together?
GOD: I thought it was going to happen. Max lives in Croton. That's only two towns over. I figured they'd run into each other sooner or later and it would be love at first sight. Guess it never panned out.
ANGEL: What about Jenny? Who is she made for?
GOD: I made her for this guy Tom, in Calgary. He loves red and purple Life Savers and she loves the citrus flavours, so if they ever bought a pack, it would work out perfectly. Also, Tom plays the violin and Jenny plays the upright bass, so if they ever wanted to jam, they could just go ahead and jam.
ANGEL: But Calgary ... that's all the way in *Canada.*
GOD: Yeah. I should have put them closer.
(Church bells ring below.)
ANGEL: Oh, no – it's too late!
GOD: That's okay. Who knows? Maybe they'll be happy.
ANGEL: Really? Is that possible?
GOD: Stranger things have happened.

A conversation between God and the man in a tin foil helmet and a Speedo who's always shouting things next to the local Aldi

– How'd it go today? Win any followers?
– I'm afraid not, God. I'm sorry.
– You told them the news, right? That the world is ending in four days?
– Yes.
– And you made the sign, like I told you? With all the information about the apocalypse?
– Of course.
– Did you try that thing I came up with, where you start swinging your arms around really fast while saying "The end is coming, the end is coming"?
– (sighing) Yes.
– And still no one listened! I can't believe this. How can I prepare mankind for the apocalypse if they ignore the words of my prophet?
– I actually had a thought today, God. I was thinking, maybe if I wore something a little more socially acceptable ...
– I have a strict dress code for my prophets: helmet, Speedo.
– Listen, God, I'm honoured that you chose me to be your prophet – and it's been a really exciting thirty-five years, don't get me wrong. But I'm starting to think that maybe you should ask someone else to deliver your message. Like a senator, maybe? Or a minister?
– Impossible. You are the prophet I have chosen.
– Well, maybe I should at least leave the shopfront of Aldi. The manager keeps sending out someone with a broom to chase me off the lot. It's pretty humiliating.
– Yeah, I saw that. That was pretty bad.
– Did you see when all the foil fell off while I was running away? So that I was completely naked, except for the helmet?

– Yeah. That probably set us back a little. Maybe you should move to the side of the highway? I'm sure we'll have more luck there.
– Okay.
– And I want you to make your sign bigger.
– Sure.
– And one more thing.
– What?
– Keep your head up.
– (Laughs.) Thanks, God.

Acknowledgments

Thanks so much to Rebecca Gray, Anna-Marie Fitzgerald and everyone else at Serpent's Tail for believing in my jokes these past ten years!

Thanks also to Dan Greenberg, Emma John, Dan Menaker and my wife, the wonderful, brilliant, beautiful Kathleen Hale.